Erin Amon

Cockapoos

Everything About Purchase, Care,
Nutrition, Behavior, and Training

BARRON'S

CONTENTS

WHAT IS A COCKAPOO?

If the name alone makes you laugh, just wait until you actually meet a Cockapoo. Their incredible personalities, adventurous spirits, and comical natures will keep you warmly entertained. Due to their popularity, the Cockapoos have many experts striving to define where they belong in the canine world. Whether classified as designer dogs, hybrids, mixed breeds, or mutts, to us, they are simply charming, lovable Cockapoos.

Cockapoos are the result of blending two wonderful breeds—the Poodle and the American Cocker Spaniel. Both breeds possess great qualities, but with the Cockapoo, we see the best of both in one lovable companion dog. The fact is that all officially recognized canine breeds are the result of human efforts to design dogs to better achieve certain purposes. Humans have worked to develop canine breeds for herding, retrieving, companionship, and protection to meet our needs. Today, design seems primarily focused on companionship. To those who pioneered the development of the Cockapoo, we can be grateful. Their efforts have brought us an amazing loyal friend and companion.

Meet the Parents

The Poodle

Through art and literature, Poodles can be traced back over 1,000 years. However, it wasn't until a striking white Poodle won the Westminster Kennel Club's prestigious honor of "Best in Show" in 1935 that their popularity exploded in the United States. The Poodle held the number one spot as the "Most Popular Dog in America" for 23 years from 1960 to 1982.

The American Kennel Club includes the Poodle on its list of hypoallergenic breeds. Comfortable living in most climates and environments, the Poodle is a great companion dog that develops a very strong bond with people. The Poodle is available in three sizes: Toy, less than 10 inches (25 cm) at the shoulders; Miniature, 13–15 inches (33–38 cm); and Standard, 22–27 inches (55–68 cm).

Excellent swimmers, Poodles were developed to work with hunters who needed dogs to retrieve waterfowl. Their pompom haircuts actually originated with hunters in an effort to improve their mobility in lakes and marshy areas. Groomers later took those cuts to distinct new levels of artistry. Poodles project a

regal countenance and observers may think they are aloof, but nothing could be farther from the truth. They are loving and eager to please their humans.

The Cockapoo inherits a great deal from his Poodle parent. The most evident trait is his size. The hypoallergenic qualities, such as odorless and low-shedding hair, are also Poodle traits. The love of water, athletic ability, high intelligence, and retrieval instincts can also be attributed to the Poodle.

The American Cocker Spaniel

American Cocker Spaniels are often described as "merry." Possessing a cheerful and friendly disposition, they are very comfortable with people, especially children. Extremely loyal and sensitive to their owners, they are assertive but easy to train. Endurance is one of the most significant physical characteristics of the intelligent Cocker Spaniel. Bred as gun dogs for hunting game on land, these strong muscular dogs need adequate exercise to remain healthy and well balanced. Their flowing silky coats will shed and regular grooming is essential for good health. The Cocker Spaniel breed standard includes a weight of approximately 25 pounds (11 kg) with a shoulder height at about 15 inches (38 cm) and docked tails.

The Cocker Spaniels' roots can be traced back as far as the 14th century to a breed referred to as "Spanyells," which is believed to have originated in Spain. In 1946, the American Kennel Club officially recognized the American Cocker Spaniel as a breed. Later named by the club as "The Most Popular Dog in America," he set a

record by holding that title over 25 non-consecutive years. Some of the physical characteristics Cockapoos inherit from the Cocker Spaniel parent are the silkiness of their wavy hair, a square-shaped muzzle, large soulful eyes, a strong muscular body, and their cheerful love of people.

History and Hybrid Genetics

Cockapoos originated in America in the 1950s. Several breeders have been crossing the English Cocker Spaniel with Poodles. However, it is important to distinguish these dogs from the Cockapoo. The English Cocker Spaniel is a completely different recognized breed with a standard and characteristics of its own. Crosses with Poodles are referred to as English Cockapoos.

Hybrids are created by crossing two known entities, such as established dog breeds. A breed is developed over generations of careful breeding until a certain ideal is well established and reproduced consistently. Detailed recordkeeping is vital to the process.

Hybrid vigor refers to the hoped-for result of a better animal, freer of the undesirable weaknesses prevalent in the parent breeds. The goal of breeding Cockapoos is to reduce congenital defects and promote certain desirable physical features.

Cockapoos have not yet achieved breed recognition, although dedicated breeders have invested many decades in working to achieve that goal. According to both the scientific and the dog fancy communities, in order to reach breed status, a minimum of seven generations of Cockapoos must be bred, producing predictable ideal physical characteristics called standards. The bloodlines must be registered and traceable to the originating hybrid pair. That may sound simple, but it is actually a very intricate process requiring an extraordinary effort. In addition, it must be accomplished multiple times, not just once.

Designing a Hybrid

The first cross of the parent Poodle and Cocker Spaniel is labeled F1. The F1's pups are Cockapoos. According to breeders, the pups are then bred to a non-related F1 and result in Cockapoo parents, creating Cockapoo pups labeled F2. Fifty percent of these offspring will lean more in appearance to either grandparent, the Poodle or Cocker Spaniel. They may not look exactly like their parents, but they are technically Cockapoos. An F2 must then be bred to an unrelated F2. Continued breeding of unrelated pairs down as far as the F7 range will eventually result in the purification of the Cockapoo line. Anytime a Cockapoo is bred back to a Poodle or Cocker Spaniel, the purity of the line is broken, resulting in pups who may be very cute and appealing, but are not *true* Cockapoos.

For the genetic map to lead to breed recognition, only the finest selection of Cockapoos possessing the most highly desired characteristics

━━━━━ TIP ━━━━━

Agility

The vigor, speed, and intelligence of the Cockapoo combine to make him an exceptional competitor in agility sports. Agility is a canine athletic sport that requires conditioning, concentration, training, and teamwork with a handler. Together, the dog and his handler negotiate an obstacle course to be judged on accuracy and speed. Visit the United States Dog Agility Association at *www.usdaa.com,* The North American Dog Agility Council at *www.Nadac.com*, and the United Kennel Club at *www.ukcdogs.com* for more details.

should be used for breeding stock. The high demand for Cockapoos has resulted in some breeders mixing bloodlines by breeding an F2 with a Poodle or a Cocker Spaniel with an F3 and so on. Some even breed back within the same bloodlines due to a lack of available breeding stock. (See "How to Identify a Reputable Breeder" on page 20 for details on how you can make sure you bring home a true Cockapoo.)

The American Cockapoo Club maintains a genetic database for Cockapoo breeders with two goals in mind. One, to further the development of the Cockapoo as a recognized breed through bloodline verification; and two, to ensure genetic testing is conducted on breeding stock to help reduce hereditary health problems. (See page 72, "Inherited Diseases and Congenital Disorders.") Enjoying the companionship of a Cockapoo will help you understand

and appreciate the efforts of the dedicated breeders and organizations who have been working diligently to develop and protect this wonderful hybrid.

Physical Characteristics

One of the most endearing physical characteristics of the Cockapoo is his enchanting face. His muzzle is more squared than pointed with a prominent nose and long hair framing his cheeks and chin. Long floppy ears set at the crown of his head hang loosely along the side of his face. His large, expressive eyes and a smile that can melt a person's heart endear him to many people.

His long soft coat is wavy or curly, not coarse or wiry. Whether the dense hair is kept long and natural or trimmed for a teddy bear look, the low-shedding, odor-free coat contributes to his immense popularity.

The Cockapoo's body is well proportioned and sturdy with a thick neck, broad chest, and strong legs capable of great speed. He can range in size from Toy, less than 10 pounds (4.5 kg); Miniature, less than 20 pounds (9 kg); to Standard, over 20 pounds (9 kg).

All recognized canine breeds are identified by a series of common and unique physical characteristics. Many breeders have been diligent in their efforts to establish a set of these characteristics for the Cockapoo. The American Cockapoo

Club, at *www.americancockapooclub.com*, adopted a physical breed standard in 2001. The following is a summary of this standard:

Size—Measured at the shoulders. Toy, up to about 10 inches (63.5 cm); Mini, 11-14 inches (28-35 cm); Standard, 15-17 inches (38-43 cm)

Tail—May be docked or left long.

Coat—The entire coat of the Cockapoo is slightly or heavily waved but never harsh, kinky or wiry. Hair on the chest, abdomen, and legs is soft and well-feathered or thick and wavy and may even be longer than the body hair.

Color—Any solid color, parti-color (two or more solid colors, one of which must be white), or tri-color (parti-color with tan markings). Brown colored dogs may have liver noses and dark amber eyes. Black, blue, gray, cream, and white dogs have black noses and very dark eyes. For the apricots and reds, the liver-colored nose is acceptable.

The characteristics described here are the result of experienced breeders, veterinarians, and other dog experts dating back to the 1960s. However, variations can occur, even within the same litter.

Personality

The Cockapoo was purposefully designed to be a devoted companion who is as comfortable living in an apartment with a single adult as he is being a member of a large family in a suburban neighborhood. Cockapoos develop deep bonds with their humans. A charming, calm,

Good Therapy

Cockapoos are well suited for work as Therapy Dogs due to their tender, affectionate natures. A Therapy Dog is trained to provide comfort to people in stressful situations, in hospitals, assisted living or nursing homes, rehabilitation centers, or schools. The dogs must successfully complete training followed by an evaluation to become certified. Details can be found at *www.TherapyDogs.com*, the site for Therapy Dogs International.

affectionate nature makes them comfortable and forgiving with children and adults of all ages. Because they thrive on human contact, Cockapoos truly are companions and should be considered "inside" dogs. He may bark to alert you to unfamiliar circumstances, such as a stranger at the door; however, he will most likely greet people with warm enthusiasm when the door is opened.

The Cockapoo is wonderfully entertaining with a comical and friendly disposition. They have playful, energetic personalities and rarely show aggression toward people or other animals. Their keen intelligence makes them quick learners. Having abundant interest in the world around them, they thrive on new experiences. They possess great self-awareness, patience, and

loyalty. A Cockapoo will demonstrate his deep affection for his humans through tender physical contact, such as cuddling beside you in a chair, curling up in your lap, or nestling at your feet on the floor.

The Hypoallergenic Facts

"Hypoallergenic" does not mean free of allergens; it means fewer allergens. It is true that Cockapoos are exceptionally low-shedding dogs; it is also true that all dogs shed. It is the hair and skin dander from a pet that tends to cause allergies among people. Many small pure breeds are known to be prone to troublesome skin conditions, which could result in more dander in their environment.

The Cockapoos are a great choice for sensitive individuals because they are low shedders and are not prone to skin conditions. The density of their hair actually helps to protect their skin. Their hair is wavy or curly, holding loose hairs in place. Normally, a Cockapoo must be brushed to remove his shed hairs. This means less hair will fall in the environment because you can control where the brushing is done.

Ultimately, it comes down to the individual person and the individual dog. For people who are prone to allergies, even dog saliva can create a problem. A person could be fine around one dog, yet have a reaction from another of the same breed. Among breeders, the Cockapoo is always included in the list of top hypoallergenic dogs.

CHOOSING AND FINDING YOUR COCKAPOO

Purchasing your Cockapoo can be as easy as going to a pet store or kennel, making eye contact with the sweetest pair of eyes you have ever seen, and writing a check. However, this is an emotional purchase and research has shown that many of these impulse purchases end up in shelters because the owner was not prepared for the responsibility of pet ownership. The best way for you to ensure you get a healthy dog with all the physical and personality traits you expect is to be prepared and well informed before you start looking. This chapter will help you decide where, when, and how to find the right Cockapoo for you and your family.

Important Things to Consider

You believe you want a Cockapoo but are you ready for the responsibility; the 15- to 20-year commitment and the investments in money, time, and patience required to add a new member to your family? Your new pup will look to you for his care, feeding, training, exercise and well-being. Are you ready to housebreak a puppy, clean up accidents, and rearrange your schedule to accommodate him? Are you willing to help a grown dog adjust to a new environment, routine, and family? Most

Cockapoo owners will tell you that all of these responsibilities are well worth the investment.

Ages of Children

If you have children, you want to make sure that they are also ready for a new member to be added to the family. Caring for a dog can teach children many responsibilities. Are they old enough to share in the daily care of your new pet? Are they too young to play with him without possibly getting hurt? Cockapoos will look at small children as playmates in the pack. A baby or young child could injure a puppy by not understanding how to handle or play with him.

——— T I P ———

A Bad Idea

A Cockapoo should never be given as a gift to someone, especially someone who does not expect it and is not fully prepared for the responsibility of caring for and owning a pet.

Children themselves can be scratched, gnawed on, or knocked over by a playful pup. Cockapoos are wonderful with children and make great childhood companions. With a little common sense and proper supervision, your children and your Cockapoo should get along wonderfully.

Potential to Show

Are you looking for a competition show dog? Cockapoos are not yet recognized as a breed by the American Kennel Club (AKC) or the United Kennel Club (UKC). If you have dreams of showing your dog in a dog show, the Cockapoo is not the right dog for you. There are, however, Cockapoo clubs, sporting events, and agility competitions that you can participate in with your dog. Beginning in 2010, the AKC will offer stand-alone mixed breed agility, obedience, and rally events.

Puppy or Adult

Which is better for your family, a puppy or an adult Cockapoo? There are several things to consider before you make your decision.

Everyone loves puppies. It's almost impossible to resist a fluffy, furry butterball with that sweet puppy breath. But puppies require a lot more care and attention than adult dogs. Puppies need to be fed more frequently, taken outside to "potty" more often, and monitored more closely than adult dogs.

A mature, healthy, well-socialized dog is more settled than a puppy. He has grown into his size, color, and coat so you know exactly what he will look like. He may be housebroken already, have a calmer disposition, and know some basic commands. If you don't have the time or schedule to commit to a puppy, an adult dog may be the way to go.

Adult dogs can be adopted for less money than you will spend on a Cockapoo puppy purchased from a breeder and will more than likely already be spayed or neutered. Unless you plan to breed your Cockapoo, you may be responsible for getting your new puppy spayed or neutered. This is an added expense to consider, but should definitely be done for health and behavioral issues with either a puppy or an adult dog. (See page 71 for "Spaying and Neutering.")

Many new dog owners think that adult dogs will not form bonds as well as puppies. This is not the case, especially with Cockapoos. Regardless of his age, he will be very loyal to his master and family. The Cockapoo loves people. His intelligence and playful disposition will help the adult dog quickly become a valued member of your family.

Bad habits can be picked up and learned by either puppies or adult dogs. Teaching good habits to a puppy will be easier than breaking bad habits in an adult dog. It may take longer with an adult dog, but there are many ways to correct behavioral issues in both puppies and adult dogs.

Whichever you decide, puppy or adult, making a Cockapoo part of your family will bring

you hours of enjoyment and a lifetime of great memories. Your Cockapoo will quickly become an irreplaceable member of your family.

Male or Female

Similar to humans, male and female Cockapoos have differences in physical traits, personality, and behavioral characteristics. Once a Cockapoo has been neutered or spayed, the differences diminish greatly. Both male and females are equally loving and loyal, with no differences in playfulness, intelligence, devotion, or desire to please their human master.

Male Cockapoos can be larger than their female counterparts. They typically have larger heads and bigger feet. Male hormones play a big part in dominance and marking behaviors, as well as an urge to roam. Once neutered, the urge to roam is diminished. Male Cockapoos have lots of energy. They are surprisingly strong and very fast. Males can form deep bonds with various family members, including relatives who visit frequently.

Female Cockapoos are slightly smaller in size. They tend to form a closer bond with one family member, but remain affectionate and attentive to everyone. Females are a little less rambunctious, but they are just as athletic as males when it comes to playing, swimming, or agility sports. Some dog trainers believe that female Cockapoos are easier to train because they are more alert and focused than males. An unspayed female may show an increase in possessiveness and sensitivity when she reaches puberty. Once spayed, however, she will become calmer and her carefree playful nature will return.

Regardless of gender, focus on the health, temperament, and personality of your potential new family member. Both female and male

Cockapoos enjoy fetching, running, playing, going for walks, lying on your lap, and having their tummies rubbed!

Where to Find Your Cockapoo

By now you have decided that the Cockapoo is the perfect dog for you and your family. You are prepared to begin your search for a healthy, well-tempered pet. Whether or not you want a puppy or an adult dog will determine where you find your Cockapoo.

Finding a Healthy Puppy

Reputable breeders are the recommended resource for purchasing your Cockapoo puppy. Most of these breeders will have an established Internet presence and be listed with Cockapoo clubs and organizations. Earning the privilege to be included in the breeder listings for these organizations is not an easy task. Breeders must adhere to strict health and breeding practices to be considered. The American Cockapoo Club lists registered breeders by type of dog and by state. Contact information, including breeder websites, is also listed. The Information Section at the back of this book provides website addresses and contact information for this organization.

Begin your search by putting together a list of breeders in your area. If there are no breeders listed in your local area, plan to visit an out-of-state breeder. Be careful of backyard breeders. An accidental pregnancy may or may not result in a pure and healthy Cockapoo. You are not purchasing a stuffed animal; you are adding a living, breathing member to your family, who will be with you for a very long time. Traveling to different breeder's kennels several

times may be necessary. (See page 22 for "Important Things to Observe" and "Important Questions to Ask.")

Pet stores are another resource for finding your Cockapoo puppy. Call several pet stores in your area to see what they have available and whether or not they are expecting Cockapoo puppies in the near future.

If you find a Cockapoo puppy at a pet store, ask to see the parents' information and ask how they acquired the puppy. Confirm the pup has had all age-appropriate vaccinations and is free of any diseases. Most reputable pet stores will share this information with you and will even guarantee your purchase.

Healthy Cockapoo puppies come from quality parents and good breeding practices. Whether you find your puppy at a breeder or a pet store, you should be diligent in your research, ask questions, and leave your emotions at home.

Finding an Adult Cockapoo

Rescue groups and shelters are the best places to find an adult Cockapoo. Not only will you be saving a life, but you will be supporting the efforts of the rescue organization. Unfortunately, pedigree, genetic makeup, and age may not be available for the rescued adult dog. There is no guarantee the dog that looks like a Cockapoo actually is a Cockapoo. Poodle rescues often include Poodle hybrids and should be included in your search.

Start your search on the Internet. Visit *www.petfinder.com* for a list of available adult

TIP

Breeder vs. Puppy Mill

What is the difference between a reputable breeder and a puppy mill? The reputable breeder will be more interested in producing a healthy quality Cockapoo. The puppy mill is more interested in producing a large quantity of Cockapoos without regard to the dogs' health or welfare.

Cockapoos that are ready for adoption from individuals or rescue groups. Contact the owner, rescue group, or shelter and follow the "What to Ask" guidelines later in this chapter to help minimize your adoption risks.

How to Identify a Reputable Breeder

A reputable breeder will have a business license (if required by state law), a breeder's contract, and a health guarantee for their puppies. The parents will be healthy and will have been screened for congenital diseases found in either Poodles or Cocker Spaniels. (For more information on congenital diseases, see page 72.)

What to Ask the Breeder

These questions will help you determine if a breeder is reputable:

✔ How long have you been breeding Cockapoos? A reputable breeder will easily discuss his history. The longer a breeder has been in business, the more knowledgeable they will be about breeding Cockapoos.

✔ Are you a member of any breeder organizations or Cockapoo clubs? The answer should be yes and the breeder should readily share this information.

✔ Do you have several references you can provide of past clients? References should not be a problem. A reputable breeder will be proud to provide you information to contact previous clients.

✔ Was this litter planned? Were the parents screened for any congenital diseases that may affect the offspring? The breeder should share genetic background information for both parents.

✔ Do you follow the breed standards of one of the Cockapoo breed clubs? Ask this question if it is important to you to know whether or not you are purchasing a first-generation, multigenerational crossbreed, or a multi-generational puppy that meets the breed standards determined by a breed club.

✔ How many litters do you produce a year? Be wary of breeders who breed more than three litters a year. Puppy mills are known for producing large numbers of litters in a single year.

✔ How many different types of dogs do you breed? More than two may indicate a puppy mill.

✔ Do you guarantee the health of your puppies? Most reputable breeders will guarantee the puppy's health for a certain amount of time and offer a refund or replacement should certain defects be found.

✔ Will you provide me with a copy of the puppy's health record? All puppies should have been examined by their veterinarian, begun their vaccinations, and been treated for worms before eight weeks of age.

✔ Do you have a contract? The reputable breeder should have a contract that sets forth the guarantees, the agreed-upon price, and any

special considerations. This is your Bill of Sale. Be sure you understand it and if not, consider having an attorney look it over.

✔ What is expected of potential buyers? Reputable breeders want to place their puppies in good homes. They are concerned about your needs *and* making sure that their dogs find safe and happy homes. Many breeders will require a deposit to hold a puppy and to ensure that a buyer is serious about the purchase.

✔ When can I visit your kennel? This is a deal breaker. No Cockapoo should be purchased sight unseen or shipped like a piece of cargo. A rep-utable breeder will gladly make an appointment for you to visit his or her kennel.

Visiting the Kennel, Rescue, Shelter, or Pet Store

Whether you are visiting a kennel, rescue home, shelter, or pet store, your objective is three-fold. First, you will want to observe everything—the facility, the operation, the own-ers, the kennel, and the dogs. Second, you will want to ask questions about the specific dog or puppy. And third, you will want to examine the

dog or puppy closely. You want to make a rational decision, not one based only on emotional responses.

Important Things to Observe

✔ Are the owners or employees willing to show you around the facility? Their demeanor and willingness should be agreeable.

✔ Are there unpleasant odors? A clean environment is a healthy environment. Some odor is to be expected, but it shouldn't be overpowering. Your puppy should come from a place that is clean.

✔ Are the puppies kept with their mother? If the puppies are kept inside the breeder's home with their mother, they have probably received early socialization with humans and other animals, which is beneficial to their future behavioral development. If the puppies are kept outside in a kennel with the mother, the pups must have socialization with people through frequent daily contacts.

✔ Inspect the parent dogs, if available, and their kennels first. Inspect the puppies last. It is hard to be objective once you have interacted with adorable puppy Cockapoos. The parents should be happy with an attentive temperament, healthy, and clean with thick, shiny coats. The puppies should be playful, adventurous, clean, and healthy with soft, shiny coats.

Important Questions to Ask

What do they know about the dog's past? Ask this question if you are adopting a dog from a shelter or rescue group. They should have some background information on the dog. Breeders should be asked about the parents and the litter registrations with professional breed clubs or organizations.

✔ What is the dog's personality and temperament like? What social skills has the dog displayed? The breeder, current guardian, or shelter employee should have interacted and observed the dog enough to know the answers to these questions.

✔ What kinds of exercise do the dogs get? Any dog, whether adult or puppy, should be given time outside a cage or kennel to exercise.

✔ Has the dog learned any obedience commands? Ask for a demonstration if the answer is yes to see how you can use these commands with the dog.

✔ What vaccinations has the dog received and has the dog been spayed or neutered? Most rescue groups make certain that these procedures are taken care of immediately. Shelters may not have the resources available to handle these matters.

✔ What is the dog's behavior like with other animals and with strangers? These behaviors should have been observed by the breeder, rescue group, or shelter employee.

It is important that you ask as many questions as you can to learn about your potential new family member. Don't be afraid to ask any question. The more you ask, the more your genuine interest in choosing the right dog for you shows.

Examining Your New Cockapoo

Once you have selected the dog or puppy you think is right for you, perform a pet examination. The pet exam begins with physical inspection and ends with the temperament or disposition of the dog.

✔ Do you see any external parasites (such as fleas or flea eggs) or any skin discolorations (such as hair loss or red spots)? If a pup has any signs of external conditions or diseases, the odds are it will have some internal ones, as well.

✔ The coat should be clean, free from mats, and shiny. Notice the markings and color of the dog. In puppies, this may or may not be indicative of the adult colors. Puppy coats will lighten as they grow older, but adult Cockapoo colors will be well established. Color shouldn't be your primary concern; there are more important factors to consider.

✔ Examine the eyes and ears for any discharge. The eyes should be bright with a friendly expression. The ears should have no odor and no signs of scratching or redness that may indicate an infection.

✔ Examine the nose, making sure it is not runny.

✔ Check the teeth and gums for redness and discoloration or missing teeth.

✔ Check the dog's body. He should appear sturdy and evenly proportioned. The stomach should not be bloated or distended.

✔ Watch the dog walk and run. Is his tail up? Wagging? Does the movement appear normal or is the dog limping? Does the dog favor one leg? Any abnormal movement could be a sign of injury, disease, or birth defect.

✔ Observe the dog's temperament. He should be friendly, alert, eager, and curious with a wagging tail. There should be no signs of aggression or extreme shyness.

✔ Pet the dog. How does he react to your touch? Most dogs love being petted and Cockapoos are no different. As you pet him, move your hands along his body then down his legs and paws. If he growls or tries to pull away when you touch a specific part of his body, stop petting. This could be a sign of injury or congenital disease. It can also mean that the dog has a fearful or aggressive temperament.

✔ How interested is the dog in you? Is the dog fearful? Easily distracted? These can be signs of extreme behavioral issues, either dominance or submission. A healthy response to you is one where he is curious, interactive, alert, and playful and shows no fear of humans.

✔ Is there a connection between the two of you? Above everything else, your personalities should be compatible. This will help ensure a happy home for you and your new Cockapoo.

COCKAPOO HOMECOMING, BE PREPARED!

Whether you adopt your Cockapoo from a shelter, pet shop, or breeder, the experience will be unsettling for your new pup. Adult dogs and puppies need special care from their new owners during these very important first days together. The most significant thing you can give your new canine companion is patience. The dynamics of your life and home will change greatly as you make him a part of your family. For your pup, however, the entire universe as he knows it is changing. In this chapter, you will find advice on preparing your home and family for some of the necessary adjustments that lie ahead.

Puppy Proofing Your Home

The Safe Zone

Before bringing your new Cockapoo pup home, locate a "safe zone" inside your house. A screened porch, kitchen, hallway, or similar area where you can see each other is best. This should be an area where, although he is contained, he can still see, hear, and be a part of normal activities in your home. Use expandable gates or pet playpens to create barriers where necessary. The safe zone should be open to daylight and large enough to accommodate your Cockapoo's growth. The floor surface should be one that will be easy to clean until housebreaking is complete. It is highly recommended that his crate be kept in this area in the daytime during his introduction to his new home. For the first couple of weeks, you may be moving the crate at night depending on the method of housebreaking you have chosen to implement. (See chapter on Crate Training and Housebreaking.)

Examine the area to eliminate choking hazards, electrical cords, or other things that might cause harm to a curious, chewing puppy. Your pup may try to eat anything he finds from insects and rocks to doorstops and dryer lint. There are safe products on the market that you can spray on furniture and other places to discourage chewing. Objects like plants or plant stands can be pulled or knocked over by a playful dog, causing him injury. An adventurous pup may even open cabinet doors so be cautious about where you store cleaning agents and harmful chemicals. Trash cans are great temptations for a dog (including those with lids attached) and should be removed from the safe zone. Many foods and plants are potentially lethal for dogs. Please review the warning on the facing page for a list of some common hazardous substances.

The safe zone should be a happy, secure place for your dog; it should never be a place of punishment. Before introducing your pup to all areas of your home, spend an hour in the safe zone playing with him. Keep certain toys only in the zone so your Cockapoo enjoys returning to his space. This is also where he should experience his first feedings. Introduce him to his crate in the safe zone. As he gets older, you can permanently remove the crate from the safe zone and replace it with a cozy sleeping mat.

The safe zone principle is similar to using a crate, but it provides more physical space, allowing for growth and interaction while keeping your pup and your home safe and secure. This is not intended to be a permanent modification of your home. As your Cockapoo matures and responds to your training commands, learning acceptable and unacceptable behaviors, the safe zone may become less necessary. However, for many people and pups, it provides safety and peace of mind when close supervision is not an option.

Beyond the Safe Zone

The rest of your home is equally important when it comes to safety. Room by room, check for things on the floor, as well as anything your Cockapoo can stretch up to reach. A few pennies left on your nightstand can cause zinc poisoning. Ibuprofen or something from a trash can dropped on the floor may result in a rush to the veterinarian's office. There are many ways to minimize potential dangers in advance. Here are a few more items to be wary of:

✔ Objects on tables (breakable items, candles, books, pens, paper, wallets, jewelry)
✔ Houseplants or silk arrangements
✔ Plug in night-lights and air fresheners
✔ Closet or bathroom doors left open
✔ Electrical and drapery cords
✔ Open windows with loose screens
✔ Briefcases or backpacks
✔ Items under the bed
✔ Throw rugs
✔ Children's toys

Outside Areas

If you have a deck or screened porch, be aware that dogs have been injured when tags on their collars become lodged in the gaps between deck floorboards. The spaces in deck railings also pose a risk of falling or for collars getting wedged. If you have a grill, check to see that it cannot be pulled over easily. When you are preparing to cook, don't leave raw meat within reach of your Cockapoo.

In the yard, be aware that a dog can absorb chemicals like fertilizer, weed killer, insecticide, and poisons through his paws and skin. Check labels for pet safety precautions.

If you have a swimming pool, keep all chemicals stored out of reach of your dog. Chemicals *properly* balanced in the water are not harmful to Cockapoos. Make certain you have adequate

means for your pup to easily crawl out of the pool and teach him how to exit safely.

Toxic Plants, Shrubs, and Foods

The following table lists common flowers, plants, and foods to avoid. Most veterinarians will have information available for you at their offices. The American Society for Prevention of Cruelty to Animals at *www.aspca.org* provides a comprehensive list online.

Warning! Toxic to Dogs!

Foods: onion, avocado, chives, grapes, chocolate, coffee, caffeine, tea, raisins, macadamia nuts, salt, garlic, candy, gum, milk, cream, alcohol, carbonated or energy drinks, bacteria in some meats and rodents

Plants: Autumn Crocus, Azalea, Black-Eyed Susan, Buttercup, Ivy, Caladium, Daffodil, Hyacinth, Hydrangea, Iris, Mistletoe, Mountain Laurel, Philodendron, Poinsettia, Rhododendron, Yew, Tobacco, Tulip, Wisteria, Yellow Jasmine, some fungi, and mushrooms

This is a partial list. Complete lists are available from your veterinarian or *www. petpoisonhelpline.com*, the pet poison helpline.

Establishing the Rules

Consistency is essential. All family members must know and participate in enforcement of the rules. A lack of consistency will lead to confusion and frustration for you and your Cockapoo.

Is the furniture off limits or not? Where will you locate the outdoor *potty spot*? What type of snacks will be allowed? How will the feeding plan be implemented? Under what circumstances will your pup be allowed off-leash outdoors? When it's time for walking, who will be responsible for taking your Cockapoo outside?

Most importantly, establish what words you will use with your dog for identifying bad behavior and what methods are acceptable for reward and correction. What words will mean "Go potty" and "Meal time?"

In order for your pup to understand and learn what is expected of him, he must receive consistent directions and responses from all family members. Inconsistent signals will result in inconsistent behaviors and confusion. Your Cockapoo is smart enough to learn that he can get away with some bad behaviors around one family member and not others if the rules are not equally enforced.

The Bare Necessities

What Puppies Need

Once you have established the rules and prepared a safe zone, it's time for purchasing supplies. This is a list of items you should have on hand when you bring your new Cockapoo puppy home:

Food and water bowls—Look for bowls small enough that your pup can easily reach over the edges to the contents inside. Slide-resistant bottoms are best.

Food bowl mat—These items help prevent bowls from sliding and protect floors.

Food—If you purchased your puppy from a breeder or pet store, they should supply you with the brand name of the food your Cockapoo has been eating. He will be dealing with a lot of changes when you bring him home. This is not the time to introduce new foods.

Bedding—A crate with a floor cushion, a settle mat, or a dog bed with bolstered sides.

Collar and leash—Puppies need lightweight collars with small clasps. Never use metal chain collars or metal leashes with young pups.

Identification—A lightweight aluminum or plastic tag with his name and your phone number is a necessity. If your Cockapoo has a microchip, include the phrase "Scan my chip" on his tag.

Toys—Be very selective. You may pay more for a good, long-lasting chew toy, but it is worth it to avoid your puppy ingesting something that could result in a trip to the veterinarian's office. Only a few are necessary at first.

What Adult Dogs Need

Adopting a more mature dog will present you with some different considerations. Does your Cockapoo's age or health prohibit or require anything special? Are there any medications he needs? Is he accustomed to a crate? If he is not, crating him now may be interpreted as punishment, as opposed to his secure, cozy den. (See the Crate Training and Housebreaking chapter for details.) Are there any known foods that previously caused him problems? Consider this basic starting supply list:

Food and water bowls—Look for bowls large enough to hold a full meal and plenty of water.

Food bowl mat—These help prevent bowls from sliding and protect floors.

Food—Whether adopted from an individual or rescued, your Cockapoo will be accustomed to eating the food he was recently provided. Keep him on the same diet for a few weeks before making any changes. As he adapts to his new home, new foods may be considered. (See "Food and Nutrition," beginning on page 43, for more on introducing new foods.)

Bedding—A crate with a floor cushion, a settle mat, or a dog bed with bolstered sides. For older dogs, a special orthopedic type bed may be necessary.

Collar and leash—Cockapoos do not need heavy choke collars. Choose a comfortable nylon or leather collar.

Identification—A permanent tag listing your phone number and his name is a must. If your Cockapoo has a microchip, include "Scan my chip" on his tag. Some microchip companies provide their phone number and your pup's chip number on a tag for you.

Toys—All dogs love a good, long-lasting chew toy, especially the ones that contain treats. Cockapoos love to chase things, tug, and fetch. Keep balls, furry animals, and rope toys in his toy basket. Toys designed to stimulate your dog's mental development will usually require him to find another object hidden inside. Be sure to ask for favorite toys he may have from his previous home or rescue center.

Introducing Your Family and Pets

What is socialization? It is "giving someone the skills required for functioning successfully in society or a particular society." That someone is your Cockapoo.

His socialization skills began at the kennel with his littermates. As soon as you bring your Cockapoo home, it's important to begin socialization with his new family pack. There are several things you can do to ensure your friendly Cockapoo learns how to behave properly with people and other animals.

Meeting Your Family Members

Introduce your new Cockapoo to one family member at a time. Do this on the floor at eye level in a confined neutral space. When the pup is comfortable, allow that person to pet, play, and pick up the puppy. If he is resistant, don't force interaction. Be patient. Reward only calm and relaxed behavior with praise and treats.

Meeting Your Other Dogs and Cats

Existing family pets are also part of the pup's new family pack. Regardless of how many other pets you have, it's important to take the time to properly introduce your new Cockapoo to each one individually.

When introducing the new pup to a family dog, make sure both are on a leash. The leash should be held loosely or allowed to drag. Start the introductions at eye level, making sure not

Its Place in the Pack

It may take several attempts at introducing a new pup to an existing family dog before they can work out where each one's place is within the pack. Letting them work this out on their timeframe instead of forcing it will help them become lifelong friends.

to give the new pup the "upper" advantage by holding him. Observe the interaction, praising the dogs, as you watch. It isn't uncommon for them to start sniffing at the nose and end at the tail. This is dog etiquette and the way dogs get to know each other. Posturing and circling is normal regardless of the dogs' sizes or ages.

Signs of acceptance include face licking, tail wagging, and the play bow (front paws stretched out in front with hindquarters raised). A prolonged direct stare, raised hackles, growling, showing his teeth, arching his body, or curling his tail between his legs are warnings of imminent fighting and require quick intervention to prevent possible injury. The dogs should be separated immediately if any aggressive behavior is observed.

Establishing dominant or submissive roles is normal and should not be confused with aggressive behavior. Signs of dominance are mounting, or placing one or both paws over another dog's shoulders, hip bumping, and raised hackles. Submissive behavior is designed to allow the dominance and is expressed by going down with head and tail lowered, or

rolling over with belly exposed. Some dogs will urinate when showing submission. Mouthing and play fighting can look and sound rough at times, but if tails are wagging and both are actively playing, all is well. There is no need to intervene unless one dog plays aggressively and the other has had enough.

Introducing the family cat requires much more caution and patience. The Cockapoo may initiate interaction a little too exuberantly. The cat's reaction will be to leave and the Cockapoo's response will be to give chase. Your pup may be afraid of the cat and try to flee. To avoid this and to let your pup and cat know that each is a part of the family, you will need to enlist the help of another family member.

Begin with one of you and the cat in a closed indoor area. The other, holding your pup loosely by his leash, should then enter. Let them approach one another on their own. Do not force either of them. The pup is most likely to initiate the meeting by sniffing and poking his nose at the cat. Praise both for this initial meeting and reward each with a treat. It could take several attempts before they feel comfortable. If either becomes aggressive, separate them and try again later. Cats and dogs rarely become companions, but they can learn to respect each other's place within the family pack.

Your existing pets have already established their roles in the family and the newcomer upsets the balance. Older pets might need more

time to adjust and shouldn't be forced to inter-
act with the new pup. However long it takes,
making sure your pets can peacefully exist
together will make life easier and more enjoyable for everyone in your family.

Peaceful Sleep and Pleasant Mealtimes

With his sweet face and happy expression,
you may forget that your Cockapoo is a canine.
Don't let that charming exterior fool you; inside
is a hungry animal. All dogs have their own
unique personalities. How each approaches his
food varies greatly. Some are very possessive
and others will happily share with your toddler.
Most fall somewhere in between.

Doggie Dining

Respect his space at mealtimes. Locate a
feeding spot that is away from distractions and
reasonably quiet. His dining area will get a little
messy when he eats and drinks so keep the
floor surface in mind. This should be a perma-

TIP

Better Eating Habits

Slow down a food gobbler by spreading
small bites of food out on a tray or place a
heavy safe object, such as a large rock, in
the center of the feeding bowl. Both of
these methods cause the dog to take smaller
bites at a slower pace.

Eventually, as feeding becomes a pleasant
routine, your pup will approach his food
more calmly and you can resume normal
food placement in his bowl. (Feeding guidelines are discussed on page 43.)

---

nent location after the first few meals in the
safe zone.

Never provide food if your Cockapoo jumps
on you or barks. Present it as a reward for
exhibiting patience until you set the food in
place for him. Preparing his food first, then

calling him to join you in the feeding area will also show him you are controlling the food.

Many puppies approach eating as if it is the last time they will ever see food, gobbling up every morsel as fast as possible. This is not abnormal, and most pups eventually slow down, but it can lead to an unhealthy condition called Bloat. (See "Inherited Diseases and Congenital Disorders" on page 72.)

A Quiet Place

Cockapoos will sleep almost anywhere when the feeling strikes them; however, all dogs need a quiet place that belongs to them, especially at night. Many people use a crate for their dog. The crate becomes a safe den to sleep in or retreat to when the home environment gets too overwhelming with noise, people, or activity. Others choose to have dog cushions in multiple rooms. Another popular option is a settle mat, which can be moved from place to place.

Settle mats provide pups with a familiar spot for resting in any location.

Your Cockapoo will naturally want to be near you at night. His quiet place should be close to where you sleep. There should be adequate warmth in cold weather and cool ventilation when it's hot.

Young pups need things to cuddle up against, things like soft blankets, furry toys, or even an unwashed T-shirt of someone in the family. Provide him a safe chew toy. Be cautious about stuffed toys; pups can chew off the eye and nose buttons and may choke. Restless puppies can be calmed by the sound of a radio, ticking clock, or soothing sound machine placed nearby.

Healthy sleep is vital for humans and dogs. Making decisions and planning ahead is extremely important, especially if your Cockapoo is a puppy. He needs the security of knowing you are next to him. You are his provider, protector, and parent.

SOCIALIZATION, EXERCISE, AND PLAYTIME

On his second birthday, a new puppy will be the equivalent of twenty-one human years old. This is why it is imperative that we teach our dog good social skills and provide him with a healthy, balanced lifestyle right from the start.

It is important that we teach our dog good social skills, especially in the first four months. Socialization means developing the skills necessary for companionship with others. It is essential for successful participation within a family or society.

Cockapoos thrive on meeting others, both humans and canines alike. One bad experience, however, may result in unwanted behaviors, which are difficult to overcome. Following the guidelines in this chapter will help you learn how to help your Cockapoo stay healthy and happy and be well socialized.

Socialization with Other People and Their Pets

The American Kennel Club introduced a program called "Canine Good Citizen Training." Your Cockapoo can earn a certificate if he can perform several good behavior skills while near other people and dogs. You can teach these skills or a local AKC-approved Evaluator/Trainer can assist you with these important basics. All dogs, including designer breeds, are encouraged to participate. Search for details at *www.akc.org* for more information.

Take your Cockapoo for daily walks in the neighborhood or park where he can encounter other dogs. When he sees another dog, he will undoubtedly want to meet and greet him by pulling, barking, or trying to run toward the dog. Restrain him until the dog and his owner approach.

Don't assume that the other dog is friendly or that the stranger wants to stop to let the dogs meet. Ask the owner if it's okay to approach. Many dogs and owners are agreeable to socializing. When the two pups are close, they will proceed with their instincts and dog etiquette by sniffing noses and tails. This will determine if they will tolerate each other.

In most cases, their tails will wag and they will show signs of friendship.

Occasionally, dogs will not tolerate each other and may growl, snarl, or start to fight. If this happens, control your Cockapoo by pulling him back with the leash and walking away. Most well balanced dogs will enjoy meeting each other, but successful interaction begins with you. Teaching your dog basic obedience is vital to natural encounters with others while walking outdoors.

Socialization with people, pets, and places will continue throughout your pup's life. Take him for rides in the car, to stores or cafés where dogs are allowed, to dog parks, and on play dates with other dogs. Teaching acceptable behavior allows you to take your Cockapoo on outings often. It will help him become an outgoing and well-behaved dog in any situation.

TIP

Good Boy!

The Canine Good Citizen Test, as adapted from the AKC.
- Accept a friendly stranger
- Sit politely for petting
- Be nicely groomed
- Walk on a loose lead
- Walk comfortably through a crowd
- Sit and stay in place on command
- Come when called
- Acceptable reaction to another dog
- Acceptable reaction to sudden distractions
- Accept separation

Essential Exercise

Exercise is "physical activity and movement, intended to keep a person or animal fit and healthy." For your Cockapoo, regular exercise is essential. An active lifestyle is as beneficial to a dog as it is to a person. Exercise improves muscle strength, burns excess calories, and promotes good cardiovascular and digestive health. Your Cockapoo is eager and happy to expend his abundant energy through exercise. Be active and participate in your pup's exercise routine.

Walking for Exercise

At first, indoor play and housebreaking activities offer plenty of exercise. As your pup gradually requires more activity in the next few months, short, playful, 15- to 25-minute walks on a leash are fine. Until he is at least 16 weeks old, be very cautious about exposure to public areas, especially where other animals may have been. You will want your Cockapoo to have a fully developed immune system before encountering a germy world. The playful walks will turn into more rigorous exercise as he matures and you should be ready to pick up the pace.

Keep in mind that over-exercising a puppy or young adult Cockapoo can lead to injury. Delicate bones and joints may suffer impaired development or result in future painful orthopedic problems. Be wary of allowing your pup to climb on stairs unsupervised or jump up onto furniture. Simply jumping up or down from furniture can cause harm to immature, growing limbs.

Leisure Walks

A puppy is consumed and fascinated with everything around him. Let him explore the sights and scents along your short walk. If he has a sudden fright, maintain a normal relaxed atti-

tude and offer controlled vocal reassurance. Be wary of over-coddling your pup or he may think fearful behavior is what you desire from him.

These early walks are crucial to your Cockapoo's emotional development and his responses to certain experiences in an unpredictable world. The things, people, and dogs he encounters will leave lasting impressions. The following is a partial list of some common things your pup may be startled by when he first sees them. Be prepared to make these positive experiences.

- People of various ages, sexes, sizes, and races
- Uniforms, costumes, or hats
- Crowds
- Wheelchairs, strollers, shopping carts, scooters
- People with canes, crutches, or walkers

of age. Your Cockapoo will eagerly want and need more exercise. If he is a Toy size (7 to12 pounds), increase the distance or time a little each week. If your Cockapoo is Miniature size (13 to 20 pounds) or Standard size (over 20 pounds), this is the time to really speed up and walk with *exercise* in mind. Walk with an increased steady pace and limit his exploration stops to either the first or the last half of your walk. Pause if your pup insists on a potty stop then pick up your pace again once he is relieved.

Walking is the best *routine* exercise your Cockapoo and you can enjoy on a daily basis. The length, distance, and daily frequency should be adapted based upon the age, health, and weight of your pup, as well as environmental conditions. Remember, exercise is ultimately about fitness. One good long walk a day is a must. An adult Cockapoo will need two short walks or one long walk a day.

Swimming

Many Cockapoos have an inherent love of water and an amazing natural swimming skill, compliments of their Poodle heritage. The Miniature and Standard size Cockapoos exhibit the greatest affinity for water.

A pup less than six months old should be limited to short dips while being held by you. Wading is fine and may lead to him paddling into deeper water on his own. As he grows older, he will fearlessly leap into a lake or swimming pool to retrieve a toy. Your Cockapoo's funny wet face and floppy ears floating along like paddles is truly a delightful sight.

Swimming is an excellent exercise for adult Cockapoos. If you find your aging Cockapoo slowing down, consider setting up a small pool in your backyard. It should be deep enough that

- Bicycles, tricycles, skateboards, motorcycles
- Umbrellas, thunder, and lightning
- Balloons, flags, and holiday decorations
- Cars, trucks, golf carts, go-carts
- Household objects, vacuum cleaners, ironing boards, brooms
- Golf clubs, baseball bats, and other sporting equipment
- Leaf blowers, lawn mowers, hand trucks

Picking Up the Pace

You should notice a significant change in your Cockapoo's energy level around six months

he can actually swim as opposed to wade, but even wading is better than no exercise. Although age may slow him down, nothing will ever diminish his love of water. (See "Boating and Water Safety" on page 86.)

The Value of Playtime

To play is "to take part in an enjoyable activity, especially a game, simply for the sake of amusement." The value of playtime with your Cockapoo is threefold. Play is about joy, learning, and amusement. Exercise is for fitness; play is for fun. Cockapoos love playing indoors and out. Behavior training and learning tricks can be fun activities, but your will be focused on your approval and the treat more than play. Play, while extremely beneficial, is *frivolous* fun.

Dog Parks and Play Dates

Your Cockapoo will have lots of energy and love to run. Whether fetching a tennis ball or Frisbee, running with another dog, chasing you or being chased by you, he will run until exhausted. Dog parks are excellent places to let your pup run and can be a fun experience for both of you. Many parks have separate areas for large dogs so your pup's playmates will be more his size. If your dog park is not fully enclosed, never let him out of your sight if you decide to take him off leash. Don't allow him off leash in public until he masters the *come* command. Veterinarians recommend all pups have their initial set of vaccines prior to exposure to public places like dog parks.

Play dates with other dog owners is also a great idea. This is especially true if you are a single owner, have no children at home, or if your Cockapoo is your only pet. Play dates most often occur at a dog owner's home. Always provide supervision when your Cockapoo is playing with another dog. The dogs' play may become quite rambunctious as they express their excitement at being together. They will normally settle into each other's presence and be more relaxed in their play within a short time. No matter how friendly he may be in neutral territory, any dog may react possessively in his own yard or with his favorite toys. The same reaction may come from either dog at the arrival of family members in the play area.

The more often the playmates are together, the more comfortable they will become with each other. It is worth the investment of your time to find a good playmate for your Cockapoo. (Follow the guidelines for socializing on page 35.) If they don't tolerate each other, find another playmate.

Indoor Games

Indoor play is also vital for a dog's exercise and health. Cockapoos were not bred to live outdoors in doghouses, dog pens, or backyards. They do not fare well if left isolated for hours at a time, day after day, with limited human involvement. Their physical, emotional, and mental health rely upon affectionate interaction with humans. Indoor play can be adapted to your home and schedule. Games such as "hide and seek" and "chase and chase me" are not out of the question indoors. Your pup will chase you endlessly to recover his favorite toy. You will quickly see that his motive is not the toy; it's the joy of the chase.

A less physical game is played by getting down to your Cockapoo's level and sitting on the floor or a small stool. Roll or bounce a tennis ball or other such toy lightly against a wall. Your pup will give chase endlessly. He may learn

TIP

Toys

Have plenty of toys for your Cockapoo and introduce new ones often. Occasionally, take familiar favorites away and bring them out a week or so later. Cockapoos crave new things to discover. They will actually get bored with some toys once they have thoroughly enjoyed them.

to "fetch" playing this game. There is much less running, but your pup will play this game as long as you will. Playing at his level gives you the opportunity for more physical contact. This is a great bonding game. Be prepared for lots of affection while playing down at his level.

FEEDING AND GROOMING YOUR COCKAPOO

How can you make sure your Cockapoo lives a long and healthy life? How can you keep his coat looking and feeling good? First, you give him a well balanced diet for his physical and mental health. And, second, you take care of his body. This chapter covers the basics of feeding and nutrition and will show you why grooming is more about health than appearance.

Food and Nutrition

Your Cockapoo has very important needs when it comes to his health and nutrition. There are hundreds of dog food manufacturers who want to help you address those needs with dry, canned, or organic food and supplements. With so many different options and expert opinions, it can be overwhelming. So, where do you start? First, you need to know feeding basics, and then what to look for and what to avoid in his food.

Basic Feeding Guidelines

Provide one bowl for water and another for food and treats. Check the water bowl at least twice a day and refresh as needed. Dogs need plenty of water during the day.

Clean the feeding bowls daily. Eating out of a dirty bowl contaminated by leftover food and saliva can cause illness.

Feed your dog on a schedule. Your Cockapoo will be happiest knowing when he can expect dinner.

Do not free-feed. You need to control the amount of food your Cockapoo eats at each meal to monitor his health. Leaving food in his bowl all day for him to eat at his discretion is equivalent to leaving a bowl of spaghetti on the table for your children to eat during the day. Not only does bacteria grow and food become stale, but you have no idea how much is being eaten at a time. Free-fed dogs tend to become overweight. They can become bloated, lethargic, and may not get the nutrients

——— T I P ———

People Food?

Many canine nutrition experts and veterinarians agree on one common factor that can extend the life of your Cockapoo and keep him healthy: Never give him table scraps or people snacks. If it's not good for you, it's not good for your Cockapoo.

required to keep their metabolism at a healthy level. Free-feeding can also make house-training more difficult.

Be consistent. Cockapoos, like most dog breeds, have sensitive stomachs. It usually takes a couple of weeks for canine stomachs to adjust to food. Once you decide on a type and brand of food, continue with it unless your dog shows signs of digestive problems. These signs can include diarrhea, vomiting, gagging, and constipation. If any of these conditions last longer than 24 hours, a visit to the veterinarian is recommended.

Read the dog food label and feed the proper amount. Dog food manufacturers include feeding directions on the pet food packaging. Feed only the amount recommended by your veterinarian or the pet food manufacturer. This will be determined by your Cockapoo's age, size, and health. (See "Understanding the Label" on page 46.)

What to Feed Your Cockapoo

Dry food, canned food, semi-moist food, frozen food, and natural food are the popular pet food choices available in local markets. The major difference between each is in water content. There are minor differences in appearance, odor, convenience, and nutrient values.

Dry dog food is the food of choice for many Cockapoo owners and breeders due to its convenience, cost, and the fact that it is almost odorless. Dry food has the lowest water content (six to ten percent), making its texture crunchy. This can help reduce gum disease by minimizing tartar buildup. It is the most economical choice and comes in a variety of flavors and sizes. Dog stools will tend to be firmer and less odorous with a dry food diet.

Canned dog food is 65 percent to 80 percent water. Because of this, the nutrient value is diluted considerably, and your dog will need to eat more to get the nutrients his body requires. Tartar buildup, gas, and odorous and loose stools are all common side effects of a canned food diet.

Semi-moist is the most expensive type of dog food. Its water content is 20 to 40 percent. Semi-moist food usually comes in single-serving packets with different flavor combinations, making it convenient. Dogs like it and it isn't as messy as canned food. The downside is that it's high in sugar, artificial coloring, and preservatives. Dental disease, soft, odorous stools, gas, and weight gain can be problems associated with a diet of semi-moist food.

Frozen food and natural food diets are new options for Cockapoo owners. Both of these are expensive and not as readily available as the other dog foods. The food is made from human ingredients and will need to be kept in the freezer or refrigerator. Unless recommended by your veterinarian, human ingredient diets are not necessary. They can be time-consuming, expensive, and result in a nutrient deficient diet for your Cockapoo if not prepared correctly.

It's always best to start with the food he has been fed by the breeder or shelter. Gradually introduce the new food type you and your veterinarian choose. For a week to 10 days, mix the new food with the old to help his digestive system adjust in a healthy manner.

Life Stage Feeding

Most dog foods are made for three life stages: puppies (newborn to one year), the adult or maintenance years (one to seven years), and senior or mature (beyond seven years). Your Cockapoo's food requirements will differ depending on his age.

Puppies are constantly growing. Their metabolism is faster than that of an adult dog. They require more protein, vitamins, calories, and nutrients to ensure their bodies grow healthy. Their teeth and bones are developing, so chew-

ing and eating are necessary several times a day. They will need to eat three meals a day and have chew bones available to satisfy their teething needs.

During the adult or maintenance years of your Cockapoo's life, his feeding needs will reduce to twice a day. His body has finished

Physical Results

How will you know if you are feeding your dog correctly? His coat should be shiny, his eyes bright, his energy level consistent throughout the day (with the exception of naps), and his weight ideal for his size.

growing and maintaining his active lifestyle in a healthy manner should be your focus.

The senior or mature years of your Cockapoo's life are his slowing down years. It's important to maintain a healthy lifestyle for him. His activity level will decrease and this is the stage when obesity can occur. His feeding will eventually reduce to once a day. Remember, a slower metabolism requires fewer calories. Check with your veterinarian to determine if one meal a day or two small meals would be better for your senior.

Understanding the Label

Pet food labels are regulated by the Association of American Feed Control Officials (AAFCO), the Food and Drug Administration, and the Department of Agriculture. Understanding the label will help you manage your Cockapoo's diet.

The following is a list of important things to look for on the label:

✔ The AAFCO nutrition adequacy statement of conformance. Without this *"complete and balanced"* statement, supplements or additional nutrients may be needed. Check with your veterinarian before providing supplements.

✔ The first two or three ingredients listed should be a type of animal protein, such as beef, chicken, lamb, or fish. This tells you that the food has a higher digestible source of protein as its main ingredient. Vegetables and vitamins should be listed next.

✔ There should be an expiration date. Never use food past its expiration date.

✔ A manufacturer's name, address, and contact information should be listed.

✔ Look for natural preservatives. Avoid foods with preservatives like BHA, BHT, and propylene glycol.

Grooming Your Cockapoo

Grooming your Cockapoo will make him feel and look good, but will also help keep him healthy. Taking care of his cleanliness is a way of defending against disease. This section provides advice on scheduled grooming activities.

Daily Grooming of Your Cockapoo

Daily grooming activities start at the head and end at the tail. First, clean the eye area of any discharge. There are products specifically designed to breakdown any build-up and reduce tear stains. You can use an eyewash solution or a saline solution to clean this area. However, warm water and a cotton ball work just as well.

The Cockapoo's ear canal is long and L-shaped with hair that lines the canal and traps wax and debris. Use a canine ear-cleaning solution to clean the ear and remove any debris or wax build-up. Long hair blocking the opening should be removed with tweezers or forceps. Your groomer or veterinarian can show you how to do this.

 TIP

Ear Care

Fill the entire canal with ear-cleaning solution completely when cleaning your Cockapoo's ear. Infections begin in the lower portion of the ear canal. The solution should spill back out of the ear if you have filled it completely. Gently massage the area beneath the ear and let him shake his head. Use a soft tissue or cotton ball to wipe out any debris.

The paws of your Cockapoo's feet should be inspected and cleaned of any debris or dirt he may have picked up during his daily walks. When walking outdoors, he can absorb harmful chemicals and substances through his paws. Use a pet wipe or damp cloth to gently wipe the paws clean. A small amount of Vaseline can help condition and protect the paws.

Long hair on his rear end can trap pieces of stool. Use a brush to remove any pieces and clean the area with a damp cloth.

If your Cockapoo is sensitive to touch under his tail, the anal glands may be impacted. Glands located on each side of the anal opening are expressed naturally when your Cockapoo has a bowel movement. They can, however, become impacted, causing pain and discomfort. If this happens, your groomer or veterinarian will need to manually express the glands.

Weekly Grooming

Hair brushing will keep your Cockapoo's coat healthy and shiny, and teeth brushing will keep his mouth free from dental diseases. Brushing your Cockapoo's hair should be an enjoyable experience for both of you. Brushing his teeth will only be enjoyable for both of you if you start when he is young. Introduce brushing to adult dogs slowly and with a lot of tender, loving care.

Brushing Your Cockapoo's Hair

The coat of your Cockapoo will vary depending on his parents. His coat could be curly like

TIP

How to Remove a Mat Without Hurting Your Cockapoo

Separate the hair around the mat so you can easily get to it. Using a dematting rake, gently work the rake into the mat while grasping the hair close to the skin with your thumb and forefinger. Hold the hair tightly to minimize pulling the skin and use a sawing motion to lift out the mat. Repeat, if necessary, to remove the entire mat. Finish with a comb to remove any remaining dead hair.

a Poodle or smooth and wavy like a Cocker Spaniel. He has an undercoat and some shedding is likely. Brushing twice a week will keep his hair free from mats, reduce shedding, remove dead hair, release natural oils in the coat, and stimulate new hair growth.

Using the right tools is as important as brushing. There are tools to remove the undercoat and minimize shedding, combs to remove tangles, dematting rakes, and tools to thin the coat. You should plan on getting an assortment for your Cockapoo.

For smooth or wavy coats, start with a gentle pin brush that will not break your Cockapoo's hair. The pin brush will not remove debris or mats, so run a narrow spaced comb through the coat to make sure you didn't miss anything. If the coat has mats, use a dematting rake to work out the mats. Use a soft-bristled brush for the face area. This is a tender area for your Cockapoo.

For curly coats, start with a wide-spaced comb to remove any debris and work your way through any tangles. Combing to the skin will help remove loose hair from the undercoat. Then use a slicker brush to work out tangles, lift the curls, and leave the coat shiny and soft. If you encounter mats, work them out with a dematting rake. Use a soft brush around his face. End your session by using a small-spaced comb. The comb should go through the coat easily.

Brushing Your Cockapoo's Teeth

Brushing a dog's teeth is something that pet owners tend to neglect even though it takes only a few minutes. Without regular brushing, your Cockapoo can develop dental disease, gum infections, and other health issues.

It will take time and patience to get your Cockapoo accustomed to having his teeth brushed. Use canine toothpaste and a finger brush before introducing a toothbrush. Never use human toothpaste to brush his teeth. He may swallow the toothpaste and this can upset his stomach.

Follow the steps below to make teeth brushing a positive experience for both of you:

Use your hands and fingers to hold your Cockapoo's chin and touch his mouth and lip area. Gently lift the lips to expose the teeth. This may take several times before he cooperates.

When he is used to having your finger in his mouth, add canine toothpaste to your finger. Massage the gums and teeth for a few seconds while praising your Cockapoo. Let him lick the toothpaste and enjoy the taste.

Use the finger brush next just like you used your finger. Place a small amount of his favorite toothpaste on the brush and brush in a circular motion. Stop often to let him lick the toothpaste off his teeth.

Introduce the toothbrush in the same manner, starting at the front teeth and slowly moving to the teeth farther back in his mouth. Remember to brush the backsides of the teeth and give him frequent breaks.

Monthly Grooming

How often you bathe your Cockapoo will depend on his activities. You should plan on once a month, but no more than twice a month. A romp in the mud or encounter with something foul may require an immediate, unplanned bath. Keep in mind, however, that too much bathing can dry out your Cockapoo's skin and prohibit natural oils from conditioning his hair. (See "HOW-TO: Bathe Your Cockapoo.")

Nail care is an important part of monthly grooming. Your Cockapoo's nails grow very fast. Long nails can cause joint and paw pain and even infection. Regular filing or trimming will keep your Cockapoo's nails at healthy lengths. It's important to know where the quick is located in the nail before beginning. (This portion of the nail supplies the blood.) Cutting the quick can be extremely painful for your Cockapoo. Have your veterinarian or groomer show you the proper way to cut his nails.

There are many tools available to take care of your Cockapoo's nails. This list will get you started:

Nail clippers—scissor, guillotine, or plier types will have safety guides that show you where to cut the nail without cutting the quick.

Nail grinder or sanding tool—These rotary sanders take a little practice, but they allow you to get all the way around the quick and shape the nail so that the quick recedes.

Nail cauterizer or styptic powder—This will stop the bleeding in case you cut the quick.

Quarterly Grooming—
A Trip to the Groomer

Your Cockapoo's coat will grow just like human hair and visits to the groomer for a professional trim are necessary. Professional groomers can be expensive, but if you keep up with your scheduled grooming activities, you can keep the cost to a minimum. No matter how talented you are, keeping your Cockapoo still and cooperative while you try to cut his hair can be a challenge. Groomers are well equipped to make the process go as quickly and painlessly as possible.

Cockapoos do not have a "standard" haircut, so you can decide what type of cut you prefer. Your groomer will have recommendations, but be prepared to describe exactly what you want to avoid any surprises. A popular style for Cockapoos is the "puppy cut" or "teddy bear cut."

Finding a professional groomer will take some research and you may have to go through several before you find one you like. Many pet stores now offer grooming services. Some veterinarians and dog washing establishments also have groomers.

Just like your hairstylist, the groomer you select for your Cockapoo should have experience, certification, a business license, and a sanitary facility. All pets groomed by a professional groomer should be required to provide proof of vaccinations and flea treatments. This practice promotes a healthy environment for all pets in the groomer's care. The following list of questions will help you find a qualified groomer:

✔ What type of training have you had?
✔ Do you have any certifications?
✔ Do you have experience with Cockapoos or similar breeds?

✔ Can you pluck the hair in his ears?
✔ Can you express his anal glands?
✔ Do you hand or crate dry? Some dogs are fearful of crate drying.
✔ How long have you been a professional groomer?
✔ Do you use any type of tranquilizer? Never use any groomer who uses tranquilizers on dogs.
✔ Can I see your facility? This is especially important if you are using a groomer who works from home.

Bathing your Cockapoo can be an enjoyable experience for both of you. Depending on your dog's activity level, you may need to bathe him a couple of times a month. To keep him looking and feeling his best, you should plan to bathe him at least once a month.

Where you bathe your Cockapoo will depend on his size. You can use the kitchen sink, the bathtub, or the shower. Never leave your Cockapoo alone in the bathtub or sink. Depending on the time of year, you may want to purchase a small plastic pool and bathe him outside.

Start a bath time routine as soon as possible with your new Cockapoo. The sooner you introduce him to his bath, the more obliging he will become. If you find him unmanageable, you may need to invest in a tethering system or take him to a dog washing facility, where he can be tethered during his bath.

There are supplies you will need to have before you begin and steps you will need to follow. The steps are the same no matter what type of coat your Cockapoo has: curly, wavy, or straight. The brushes will vary depending on his type of coat, but the other supplies are the same. This is a list of recommended supplies:

✔ A tool bucket to keep his bathing supplies together.

✔ A waterproof apron. These can be found at beauty supply stores.

✔ A thick beach towel to towel-dry him and a soft cloth for the face area.

✔ The appropriate pH balanced shampoo for his skin type. There are shampoos available for dry, sensitive, hypoallergenic, and normal skin types.

✔ A tearless shampoo for the face and head area. Tearless shampoos are gentle and will not burn his eyes.

✔ A pH-balanced conditioner. Leave-in spray conditioners can be used on coarse coats to add extra shine. These also work well in between baths to freshen your Cockapoo's coat.

✔ Brushes and combs. See the section on "Weekly Grooming" for a list of the brushing supplies recommended for different types of coats.

✔ Blunt nosed scissors. Use the scissors for any trimming that is needed around his face, ears, paws, and sanitary trim areas.

✔ Cotton balls and a saline solution or tear stain cleaner for the eye area.

✔ Forceps or tweezers for removing any long hairs in the ears.

✔ Nail clippers, sanding or grinding tool, and a nail cauterizer or styptic powder.

✔ A forced-air dryer made for dogs or a human hair dryer. Never use the high heat setting on a human hair dryer when drying your Cockapoo. You can easily burn the skin and dry out the hair follicles, permanently damaging his skin.

Follow these steps when bathing your Cockapoo:

✔ Always start by brushing and combing your Cockapoo (no matter how dirty he is) to remove any debris or mats before getting him wet. Start with a wide-toothed comb, a slicker brush, or a pin brush. Brush in the growth direction of the hair and then back brush to reach the undercoat. Finish with a small toothed comb to return the hair to its correct position.

✔ Remove any mats with a dematting rake and use the same techniques you did for his weekly brushing. Water will make mats tighter and more difficult to remove, causing discomfort to your Cockapoo.

COCKAPOO

✔ Wet the coat thoroughly using cool to tepid water. Avoid getting water inside the ears. Water in the ears can easily develop into ear infections.

✔ Dilute the shampoo and lather the coat, starting with the head and moving down the body toward the tail. Lather the entire body, belly, legs, and tail. This will work the shampoo to your dog's skin, making it more effective. Avoid getting shampoo in his eyes and ears.

✔ Rinse thoroughly, starting with the head and working down the body. Be sure to remove all suds and rinse under his belly. If any amount of shampoo is left on his skin, it may become irritated and itchy. Rinse him again if necessary.

✔ Apply conditioner, starting at the head and working down the body. Massage the conditioner through the hair and rinse again.

✔ Use a thick towel to remove as much water as possible from his coat. Take him outside, if the weather permits, or into the shower and let him shake. This step will shorten your drying time.

✔ Use a hair dryer on the cool or no-heat setting. For curly hair, dry in long strokes away from the body, using your fingers to loosen the curls. For straight or wavy hair, dry close to the body and brush with a pin brush as you work your way through the hair.

✔ Once the hair is completely dry, brush and comb out your Cockapoo again.

✔ Check the eye area and, if necessary, remove any tear stains using a saline solution or warm water and a cotton ball.

✔ Trim any areas that need it with scissors. Usually, the eye, mouth, belly, rectum, private

parts, paws, and ear areas will need some trimming. Be very careful trimming around these sensitive areas. Trim long hair under the paws and between the toes.

✔ Remove any long hairs at his ear openings using the tweezers or forceps.

✔ Clip the toenails following the guidelines in the "Weekly Grooming" section. Use either the nail clipper or sander/grinder and avoid cutting the quick.

✔ Finally, spray a little pet cologne on your Cockapoo. Pet colognes come in a variety of scents. Groomers use them as a refreshing finish to a grooming session.

Your Cockapoo is now looking and feeling his best. He deserves a treat and will probably need to go outside.

CRATE TRAINING AND HOUSEBREAKING

It is often said, "Your home is your castle," but to your Cockapoo, your home is just a piece of his whole universe. To him, your home deserves no more respect than the great outdoors. He will explore it by smelling, tasting, and chewing. Then he will shamelessly answer nature's call, leaving you little packages and puddles. It's up to you to keep the peace in your kingdom. This chapter will help you teach your new Cockapoo the laws of the land.

Crate Training Considerations

Although it may seem cruel and selfish, the truth is that using a crate is one of the best things you can do for your Cockapoo and your peace of mind. If properly introduced, the crate will become his den. A dog loves being in a cozy, covered space where he can feel safe. This section explains why using a crate is one of the kindest things you can do for your dog.

The Comfort Factor—Your Cockapoo needs a refuge. He needs a place he can retreat to if circumstances in your home become overwhelming. Visitors, delivery, and repair persons coming to your home may be unsettling for him. A thunderstorm or any uncommon sound may cause him anxiety. Trained pups will happily seek the comfort and security their crates provide in these and many other situations.

Safety—Inside his comfortable crate, he is protected from anything that could cause him harm or that he might harm.

Travel—A crate is one of the safest places for your Cockapoo while traveling in a car. Many airlines allow you to carry on small dogs in plastic crates that have the "airline approved" statement on the label.

Housebreaking—Crates can be used as a tool to help train a puppy how to "hold it," which is a huge milestone on the road to success in housebreaking.

Natural Disasters and Personal Emergencies— Dogs that have been crate trained will remain calmer in these situations.

Choosing the Right Crate

Crates are categorized into three basic types.

Wire crates: These appear most like cages, with narrow metal bars on all four sides. They have a plastic tray underneath the bottom that slides out for easy cleaning. Wire crates are durable and easy to assemble. Ventilation is excellent due to the openness on all four sides.

Soft-sided crates: These are made of canvas and mesh. They are lightweight and easy to transport. When it comes to durability, some of these have a hard time standing up to chewing pups. Many dogs have chewed their way to freedom through the zippered doorways.

Plastic carriers and crates: For durability and protection from the environment, it's hard to beat the plastic crates. Although they are

warmer than the wire or soft-sided styles, most do not offer as much ventilation.

It's important to remember that the crate should be properly sized for your Cockapoo. There should be enough room for him to stand without lowering his head. He should be able to lie on his side with legs outstretched without touching the sides. Look for a crate with moveable panels which can be adjusted to accommodate a puppy's growth.

Cockapoo Meets Crate

How you introduce your Cockapoo to the crate will determine your success or failure. It will require your patience and commitment. Depending upon his age and his prior exposure to crates, the introduction process could take days or weeks.

Begin the crate introduction in the safe zone. When he is limited to this space, your Cockapoo is able to focus better. Put a soft blanket and toy inside the crate. Prop the door open so it won't accidentally close. Playfully touch the door and put your hand inside while encouraging him to join in the fun. If he enters the crate at this time on his own, praise him and give him generous affection. Do not close the door.

If your Cockapoo seems reluctant to enter the crate, it's time for treats. Place a few delicious treats just inside the door. He will take a step in to get them. When he does, toss a few deeper into the crate. His love of treats will eventually overcome his uncertainty and he will enter the crate. Praise him and give him affection, but do not close the door. Let him play with the crate door open. Encourage him with toys and treats repeatedly until any fear of the crate is eliminated.

Anytime he seems sleepy, use treats to lure him into the crate. Leave the door open and encourage him to take a nap, but do not hold him down or force him. Sleeping in his crate is a great sign of progress.

Now comes the dreaded door closing. Using favorite treats and a tired dog is the best way to make this advance in crate training. When your Cockapoo is happy inside the crate, casually shut the door and turn away to another activity. After two minutes or so, open the door without making a fuss, and return to your other activity. Repeat this process several times increasing the length of time that the door is closed as you increase your distance from the crate. If he has any anxiety, delay this step and try again later.

Your goal is to have a Cockapoo who *knows* the door is closed without feeling trapped and alone. Waking up from a nap alone with the door closed may frighten him. Make sure you are in the room with him to open the door.

Now it's time to close the door and leave the room for several minutes. Once he is settled in the crate, close the door and leave. Return after just a few minutes, avoiding any interaction or eye contact, and then casually open the crate. Repeat this several times, so he will learn to expect your return to release him. Increase the length of your absence a little each time.

If your Cockapoo begins to whine and protest after you leave the room, don't rush back in to release him. He will quickly learn that whining and yelping will result in something good. Instead, wait awhile and if he doesn't settle down, walk into the room, avoiding any interaction or eye contact. Busy yourself for a minute or two. When he has been quiet for at least 30 seconds, greet him and open the door. Reward him only when he has been quiet.

Your Cockapoo's introduction is complete when he will freely enter, stay, and sleep in the crate with the door closed.

Alternative Method. Another technique you may want to try at step two is to feed your Cockapoo in the crate. This method works well if your pup is very reluctant to enter the crate. Place his food bowl in the back of the crate at meal time. He will go into the crate for his food and develop a positive association with being inside. Repeat this feeding routine several times. Your pup will eventually go happily into his crate, tail wagging, before you even have his food ready. Once he is happily eating in his crate, you can close the door. When he has finished, wait at least two to three minutes, then open the door. Repeat this process for each meal, leaving the door closed longer each time. Build on this by leaving the room while he is eating, gradually increasing your absence each time. The only drawback to this method is that your Cockapoo may expect a meal while in the crate, regardless of the time of day, even at bedtime.

House-training

Without a doubt, this is the most important training you will provide your Cockapoo. With your clear directions and consistency, he will learn where he is allowed to relieve himself (his potty spot).

An adult Cockapoo may already be housebroken; however, you may experience a few accidents as he is learning his new environment. It could take a few days or a couple of weeks before he fully adapts to your home and understands where his new potty spot is located. If he has an accident, never punish him.

A puppy will require your greatest effort because until he is approximately four months old, he may need to go as many as 12 times a day. Follow these guidelines to help ensure success:

First, select a potty spot. An area close to your home that is easy for you to access on cold rainy days makes a good spot.

Place a scent lure at the potty spot. Scent is a tremendous stimulator for a dog. There are many forms of scent lures available at pet stores, or you can use your own pup's scent by dabbing up his mess with a paper towel. The scent should stimulate your Cockapoo to take action and relieve himself in that spot.

Create a schedule. Remember, young pups need to relieve themselves when they wake up in the morning, after a nap, when they finish a meal, and after playtime. Time these activities throughout the day to include a trip to the potty spot. Maintaining a schedule will help your pup's body get into a routine.

Introduce a potty command. Many people use *hurry up, do it now,* or *go potty.* Keep it simple. As soon as your pup begins to relieve himself, speak the potty command, praise him, and give him a treat. Your pup will learn to associate the command with the action and reward. Eventually, he won't need the reward; your praise and his relief will be enough. Until your Cockapoo is more mature and successfully house-trained, never let a trip to the potty spot turn into play-time. Keep his focus on relieving himself.

Crate Method

Today, many experts feel using a crate is the fastest and easiest way to house-train. By using your Cockapoo's natural instinct not to soil his den, you are helping him develop bladder and bowel control.

With the crate in the safe zone, use it through-out the day. Go directly to the potty spot when he wakes up from his nap. Accidents may occur in the safe zone at first, but remember not to punish your pup for your mistakes. It takes only a few seconds of you looking away for an accident to occur. Use the crate with the door closed as much as possible and keep to the schedule.

Move the crate to your bedroom at night. After he is tucked in, he may rest happily for

TIP

Two House-training Rules

Clean up every accident thoroughly with an enzymatic cleaner, which will remove the stain *and the odor.* If you don't, your pup will be drawn back to the same spot to do what nature tells him to over and over.

Intervene *only* if you catch your pup in the process of relieving himself. Scolding or punishing him just seconds after he has fin-ished will only leave him confused as to why you are angry and will result in his becom-ing frightened of you.

several hours before waking up with the urge to relieve himself. Listen for any sounds or whim-pering during the night. Be prepared to quickly take him to the potty spot and use your *go potty* command. When he finishes, praise him, take him back to his crate quietly, and put him inside. The more you use the crate, the faster his blad-der control will develop, and the sooner your nights will be uninterrupted.

When you are ready to allow him more free-dom around your home, you should watch him more closely. At any sign that he needs to relieve himself, take him quickly to the potty spot.

Make a serious effort to maintain the schedule you created. Your Cockapoo will learn the rou-tines you establish. He will learn to control his urges through your consistency until he is in the proper place at the proper time.

Paper Method

Before the crate method became popular, peo-ple used newspapers or other disposable papers for house-training. Today, there are special pads available at pet stores that include scent lures and odor control elements. The bottom layer is made of plastic to minimize floor surface clean-ing. For Cockapoo owners living in urban settings, those with limited mobility, or the elderly, this alternative method has some merit. Use the papers instead of the outdoor spot. You may choose to use an indoor litter box like cat owners or progressively move the papers closer and closer to the outside door. Eventually, you will move the papers outside to the spot you chose. Be diligent about watching your pup and quick to take him outside, praising him for each success. Don't let the trip turn into playtime; it should be about relieving himself. He will learn to go to the door to alert you when has to relieve himself.

BEST BEHAVIOR OBEDIENCE TRAINING

In this chapter, you will learn how to teach your Cockapoo some basic but very important behaviors. Many experts agree that indoor house pets should always be trained using reward-based methods, as opposed to a dominance program. The reward methods are identified by enticing a behavior with a lure (the treat) and rewarding your pup's understanding and performance of the desired behavior.

Chubby Treats

Small bites of a tasty but healthy treat should be used. You will be giving your Cockapoo a lot of rewards during training so keep his health in mind. Pet stores have a variety of training treats to choose from, made specifically for healthy training. Professional trainers like using a handful of kibble (your pup's dry dog food), saving the special treats for more difficult training. We will start with the most important behavior, the *watch me* command.

Watch Me

The success of teaching new behaviors depends upon your ability to get your pup to *focus*. He must focus his attention on you long enough to understand that you expect something from him and that if he pleases you, he will get a reward. It often takes just a few seconds of his undivided attention for you to introduce him to a new behavior. In order to get his undivided attention, you will use the *watch me* command. This teaches your dog to make eye contact with you on command and alerts him to look to you for direction.

✔ Start in an area with as few distractions as possible.

✔ Have your pup sit or stand facing you.

✔ Reach out holding a treat in front of his nose.

✔ After just a second, slowly pull the treat back to your face and say, *"Watch me."*

Daily Brushups

You can easily incorporate *watch me* training into day-to-day activities. Keep a few treats in your pocket while you move about your home. As you encounter your Cockapoo in a hallway or if he follows you into another room, pause for a moment and do the exercise. Use this throughout the day as a way of mentally checking in with your pup.

✔ At first, his eyes will be glued to the treat.
✔ Repeat this until his eyes move from the treat to your face.
✔ Praise him immediately, saying, "*Good, watch me*" and give him the treat.
✔ Repeat often over the course of several days.

In time, he won't need the treat; your hand raised to your face and the *watch me* command will be enough to get his attention. However, keeping his attention on you, rather than on chasing after a squirrel, lunging at a passing dog, or jumping on a passerby, may require several treats. To prepare for these more challenging situations, training must advance to a new level. After a week or so of basic *watch me* success, it's time to add distractions.

✔ Start with the usual *watch me* exercise.
✔ Take a step to your right, saying, "*Watch me*" as you move.
✔ Keep his attention by repeating the verbal and hand signals if necessary.
✔ Once he is following you with his face (not his body), reward him.
✔ Repeat with five repetitions during each training session.

At your next training session, repeat the exercise while stepping to the left.

Over the next few training sessions, challenge your Cockapoo to *watch* you while you move. Take several steps to the right and left. You can also back away from him, enticing him to move with you as he continues watching you. Keep his excitement level high by praising him often.

The greatest challenge comes next, as you carefully begin to add larger distractions. Begin by having a family member or friend walk past you while your pup is *watching you*.

Slowly build up to more intense distractions. Have a couple of children walk by. Ask another

person to bounce a tennis ball. Next, try the command when a dog is walking by twenty feet away, ten feet away, five feet away, and then, the ultimate test: a dog going right by you.

Every Cockapoo has his own unique personality. You know him better than anyone. He wants more than anything to please you, even though he may fail at times. Use your own judgment and knowledge of his personal abilities and temperament during any training. These proven training methods should work, but be flexible and sensitive to your pup's own personality.

Good Boy, Come

After the *watch me* command, *come* is the most important behavior you should teach your Cockapoo. For him to learn this command well and to want to comply with your request, you should always keep these essential recommendations in mind.

Come must be associated only with something pleasant and positive. Always give him praise, a treat, or a few moments of one-on-one playtime.

Avoid using *come* when it's time for a trip to the veterinarian, groomer, or other less enjoyable activity. Simply walk over to him, put on his leash, and use another command, such as *let's go*.

Never say "*come*" and then scold him. Always use your happiest voice to call him to you, even if he is choosing to disobey you at the moment.

Teach the *come* command in an enclosed area until he masters it.

Never say "*come*" when your pup is running away from you. He can't make the proper association while moving in the wrong direction.

In the early stages of training, never call him when you know he is totally distracted. Set him up for success by waiting until you have his attention.

You should use different words for different situations. For example, you might want to use *crate time* when you need him there or *we're done* to get your pup moving along when he stops to sniff during a walk. Save *come* for when you expect him to walk directly to you. Follow these steps during your training exercise.

✔ Turn to face your Cockapoo, starting out close to him. Make sure he is looking at you.

✔ Start targeting (slapping your leg, making noises, and backing up). If your pup starts to move toward you, say, "*Come!*" When he reaches you, step back a few more steps and then stop. Say, "*Good boy, come*" in a happy tone of voice.

✔ If targeting isn't working, have a treat in your hand and make sure your pup can see it. Once he starts to move toward you, say,

"*Come!*" After he reaches you, say, "*Good boy, come*" and give him the treat.

✔ Tell him to *come* anytime he is coming toward you. For example, if he sees you with his food dish and is walking toward you, tell him to *come* and when he gets to you, reward him with "*Good boy, come.*"

✔ As your Cockapoo gets better at the *come* command and you feel he understands it, move further and further away. Give the *come* command before he starts moving.

✔ Add distractions once your pup is consistently following instructions.

✔ Once he is distracted, say "*come*" at the moment he can most easily disengage from his other activity; for example, when he turns away from the passerby.

✔ Add distance and distractions thoughtfully, slowly, and carefully.

Sit Boy

✔ Start with your Cockapoo facing you, holding a treat in your hand.

✔ Reach out so the treat is just above his nose, where he can smell it.

✔ Slowly move the treat up so his nose goes up to follow it.

✔ Make sure the back of your hand is touching the top of his nose.

✔ As his head tilts up, his rear will naturally go down. Just as his bottom makes contact with the floor, praise him and give the treat.

✔ Do this several times in five-minute sessions throughout two days, gradually moving your hand to a position a few inches above his nose.

✔ When your pup consistently puts his bottom down, it's time to add a verbal *sit* to build an association with the action.

✔ Continue with the five-minute sessions, always saying *sit* at just the right moment, when his bottom touches the floor, praising him and giving him the treat. Do this for a day or two.

At your next training session, stand with a treat in your hand and say, "*Sit*" before you reach out. Try not to repeat, "*Sit, sit, sit*" if it takes him a few moments. Be patient, say his name, then *sit,* and wait about 30 seconds for him to make the association.

The first time he gets it and sits, praise him joyfully and give him the treat.

Repeat this immediately at least five to seven times. Practice about five minutes at a time a few times a day.

Gradually phase out the treats and emphasize your happiness when he performs. Don't rule out the treats altogether; remember, Cockapoos love nothing more than a tasty treat.

TIP

Professional Help

If you are interested in the services of a professional dog trainer, these national organizations certify highly qualified individuals who have been certified through training and have a proven track record of success. The Association of Pet Dog Trainers at *www.APDT.com* and the Certification Council for Professional Dog Trainers at *www.ccpdt.org* are excellent resources.

I Said, "Stay"

Stay means "Stay put until I tell you it's okay to move about." For a young puppy under four months old, it is very difficult to be still for more than a few seconds unless he is asleep. Although it's never too early to try, most experts wait until a pup has mastered the *come* and *sit* behavior before challenging his overwhelming desire to move, explore, and play. When your Cockapoo is about four months of age, you will experience the greatest success with *stay*.

The *stay* behavior is so important because once your pup masters it, he finds it comforting, not confining. In an uncertain situation, when he may feel anxious, having him *sit* and *stay* helps reassure him that you, his leader, have control over chaos. He is secure in your calm instruction, knowing exactly what he needs to do.

Step One

✔ Have your dog *sit* and then say "*stay*," using a hand signal (palm facing toward your pup). The hand signal can be very effective as Cockapoos are very visual creatures.

✔ Require only a one-second stay—mark the behavior with a "*good stay.*" Reward him with a treat and then release him using the *come* command.

✔ Reward before the *stay* is broken and before you actually release him with the *come* command.

Step Two

✔ Add duration. Have him *sit* then *stay*.

✔ Wait three seconds before marking the behavior with "*Good stay*" and a treat.

✔ Continue with a few repetitions, slowly building up the time.

✔ If he pops up, ask him to *sit* and *stay* again, but decrease the amount of time for the *stay*. If your pup is breaking the *stay*, be patient and slowly build back up again.

Step Three

When your dog has mastered *stay*, you will want to add duration, distractions, and distance. Train for duration first, then add distractions, and follow with distance.

✔ Start distraction training by first having your dog *stay* in different locations.

✔ Next, add distractions that you control, for example, stretch your arms, tie your shoe, or exercise in place.

✔ Slowly build up to other distractions. Bounce a ball once at first and then build up to several bounces. Reach for something behind you.

✔ Now, add distractions you don't control, such as people walking by.

✔ Once he has duration and distractions mastered, you can add distance.

✔ Start this training by turning your back to your Cockapoo and not moving. If he *stays*, take a step away, then two, then three. Again, start slowly and build up.

✔ During your outdoor walks, stop and say, "*Sit.*" Use your hand signal and say, "*Stay.*" Take a step or two away, repeating the *stay* command. Go back to your dog and reward him by continuing the walk.

What Is Clicker Training?

A clicker is a small handheld training tool that emits a sharp click when depressed. It is used by many professional trainers and dog owners to "mark" a dog's behavior at a precise moment. The click should then immediately be followed by verbal reinforcement and reward. In this way, your pup can learn to associate the click with his last action. It helps the animal to identify exactly which of its actions or behaviors has pleased you. Clickers are available at most pet stores.

HEALTH AND WELLNESS

Your Cockapoo's healthcare is about prevention and early detection. It's about knowing what possible diseases can be inherited and what conditions can develop during his lifetime. Because your Cockapoo can't tell you when something is wrong, you will need to notice changes in his behavior and with his body. He depends completely on you for his healthcare. This chapter will help prepare you for that responsibility.

The Veterinarian— Your Partner

As soon as you bring your Cockapoo home, you will want to have him checked by a veterinarian. The veterinarian will become his physician, his dentist, and his surgeon, taking care of everything from preventive maintenance to the treatment of injuries and diseases. Finding a veterinarian you trust should be your first priority.

One of the biggest challenges for veterinarians is communicating with their patients. They have to rely on you to speak for them and to follow their instructions for the patients' care. It's critical to your Cockapoo's health for you to feel comfortable with the veterinarian you choose.

Finding the Right Veterinarian

Finding the right veterinarian for you and your Cockapoo may take a little time and effort; just like doctors, not all veterinarians are the same. The best way to find a veterinarian in your area is through recommendations. Talk to your neighbors, friends, and co-workers who own dogs. They will have firsthand experience and knowledge. Look for veterinarian clinics during your daily activities; check your local Yellow Pages *(www.yellowpages.com)* for clinics close by.

Once you have a list of names to consider, use this checklist to determine which veterinarian is right for you:

✔ Check the Internet for the veterinarian's website. You will be able to learn about the clinic, the hours and location, the doctors, and what services are offered.

✔ Call the clinic to speak with the staff. Let them know you have a new dog. They should be friendly, accommodating, and knowledgeable. Ask if you can visit the clinic and speak with the veterinarian.

✔ What are the hours of the clinic? Are they open on weekends? Do they have emergency hours or where do they refer after-hour emergencies? You will need to know where to take your Cockapoo in the event of an emergency.

✔ Do they take appointments or is the facility a walk-in clinic?

✔ How many veterinarians are at the clinic? Will you be comfortable seeing different veterinarians at a large clinic for your Cockapoo's care?

✔ Do they offer boarding, training, or grooming services?

✔ What are the costs for routine checkups, vaccinations, X-rays, surgeries, and prescriptions? How do they compare to other clinics in the area?

✔ Does the clinic accept pet health insurance? Health insurance for pets is becoming more acceptable and popular with pet owners due to the rising costs of pet healthcare. (See the section on "Pet Health Insurance.")

Visit the clinic with your adult Cockapoo before you take him in for his first checkup. This allows you to see the facility, speak with the staff in person, and familiarize your Cockapoo with the clinic before he is actually treated. If he is a puppy, leave him at home for this initial visit.

The clinic should be clean with no strong odors. The veterinarian and staff should be friendly to both you and your Cockapoo. They should answer your questions readily and allow you to walk through the facility and into an exam room.

There are probably many veterinarian clinics available in your area. Take the time to visit several before deciding which one will be the best partner for you and your Cockapoo.

The Checkup

Your Cockapoo's first checkup is important to ensure that you have purchased a healthy dog and to identify any potential health problems. Make a list of questions before your visit so you don't forget anything. The veterinarian clinic will record his weight, check his temperature, and look at his eyes, teeth, throat, and ears. They will run a fecal test and blood test to rule out parasites. They will check your Cockapoo's skin to look for signs of allergies or possible skin infections. Your Cockapoo will be checked from head to toe for any signs of concern.

The veterinarian will discuss diet, heartworm and flea treatments, and answer any questions you may have about caring for your dog. Following your veterinarian's advice is vital to the continued health of your Cockapoo.

If your Cockapoo is a puppy, you can expect several visits to the veterinarian during his first six months of life. His immune system is not fully developed at this stage, making him more susceptible to illnesses and parasites. The veterinarian will monitor his growth and continue to look for any possible health problems. Many of these health problems can be treated effectively if caught early in your Cockapoo's development.

Vaccinations

Vaccinations are as vital to your Cockapoo's health as his pet food is to his diet. Vaccines protect against infectious diseases, such as rabies, parvo, distemper, and parainfluenza, by stimulating the immune system to produce antibodies. Your pup will need to receive a series of vaccinations. The vaccinations begin after weaning and are usually started by the breeder or kennel. Let your veterinarian know what vaccines your Cockapoo has already received. The following table will give you an idea of a typical vaccination schedule for a Cockapoo puppy.

Typical Vaccination Schedule for Puppies

- 8 weeks—parvo, distemper, parainfluenza
- 12 weeks—parvo, distemper, parainfluenza, infectious hepatitis, bordetella (kennel cough)
- 16 weeks—parvo, distemper, parainfluenza, infectious hepatitis, bordetella (kennel cough), rabies

Your veterinarian will let you know the vaccinations your Cockapoo will require. Yearly boosters are needed for some vaccines and two- to three-year boosters are required for others. These vaccines will keep him protected against deadly diseases throughout his life.

Spaying and Neutering

What is spaying and neutering? Spaying is removing the reproductive organs (uterus and ovaries) from a female dog and neutering is removing the reproductive organs (testicles) from a male dog. Most veterinarians agree that spaying and neutering are healthy procedures for dogs as a preventive measure against cancer. After euthanasia, cancer is the number one killer of dogs.

Unless you are planning to breed your Cockapoo, there are many advantages to spaying or neutering at an early age:

- It reduces the risk of tumors or cancer developing on the reproductive organs. For males, neutering protects against testicular cancer and reduces the risk of prostate disease. For females, spaying eliminates the risk of ovarian or uterine cancer, uterine infections, and reduces the risk of breast cancer—if performed after their first heat cycle.

• It prevents against unwanted pregnancies. Female puppies can become pregnant as early as their first heat cycle, which may occur even before six months of age.

• It improves behavior by reducing roaming, urine marking, and disruptive sexual behaviors.

• It improves the disposition of the dog because he or she will no longer be controlled by raging hormones.

• It will increase your dog's quality of life.

• It will help decrease the overpopulation of dogs.

Spaying or neutering your Cockapoo will not change his activity level, playfulness, or energy. He or she will not miss the reproductive organs. It is a simple procedure that will improve the life span of your Cockapoo by 40 percent. Complications are extremely rare, discuss them with your veterinarian if you have any concerns.

Inherited Diseases and Congenital Disorders

You may have heard that Poodle hybrids are healthier than their purebred parents because mixing the two breeds *eliminates* the inherited diseases associated with those purebreds. However, this simply is not true. Many of these inherited diseases can be *reduced* through good breeding practices. Two healthy parents, screened for and free from hereditary diseases, are more likely to produce healthy offspring.

What are the diseases that can be inherited by your Cockapoo? According to the Atlantic Veterinarian College, any disease or condition inherited by the Poodle or Cocker Spaniel can be inherited by the Cockapoo.

The following list shows the most serious hereditary disorders that are more common among Poodles and Cocker Spaniels. These conditions require medical treatment or surgery and can affect the dog's quality of life. Talk to your veterinarian about screening your Cockapoo for these inherited disorders.

Possible Disorders

Patellar Luxation—the kneecap pops out of its groove. The dog will not put pressure on the leg while the kneecap is dislodged. It can be extremely painful. The kneecap may pop back into the groove on its own, but treatment and care will depend on how often the luxation occurs and how easily the kneecap slips back into place. Severe cases require surgery to keep the kneecap in its groove and to prevent osteoarthritis.

Hip Dysplasia—abnormal development of the hip joint. This disorder is typically not apparent until the dog is at least two years of age. Limping after an activity or avoiding activities altogether are signs of discomfort or pain. An X-ray is needed to confirm the diagnosis. With early detection, a treatment plan can be developed to relieve the discomfort. In severe cases, surgery may be necessary.

Mitral Valve Disorder—a heart valve isn't developed correctly and blood pumps back into the atrium. This condition is more often seen in small and older dogs. Dogs can live for a number of years without any problems by maintaining a healthy weight and regular exercise. As they mature, however, the heart will begin to fail. Because there is no cure for this disorder, your veterinarian will recommend the appropriate medical therapy, which may include a special diet, exercise restriction, and medication to treat the failing heart.

Sebaceous Adenitis—fatty glands on the skin become inflamed and are destroyed. This

TIP

How Can You Tell If Something Is Wrong With Your Cockapoo?

Dogs are creatures of habit. Any sudden change in your Cockapoo's normal behavior or routine can mean he isn't feeling well. Other signs include: lack of appetite, tiring easily, irritability, sleeping more, not drinking or drinking excessively, and hiding.

condition causes patches of hair loss, dry scaly skin, and, depending on the severity, secondary skin infections. There is no cure for this condition requiring long-term treatment with anti-seborrheic shampoos to remove the dry scales and dead hair, dietary supplements, and the use of oral fatty acids.

Geographic and Detached Retinal Dysplasia—abnormal development of the retina causing some loss of vision or blindness to the dog. Your veterinarian can test the dog's vision if you suspect there may be a problem. There is no treatment for retinal dysplasia; however, dogs can compensate very well for any visual impairment with their keen sense of smell and hearing.

Seborrhea Dermatitis—the outer layer of skin, glands, and hair follicles become hyperproductive, producing dry scaly skin and fatty substance. This condition causes excessive scaling, a greasy feel and odor on the skin, wax buildup in the ears leading to infection, and a thickening of the foot pads. Secondary infections and skin lesions, causing itching and scratching, are common with seborrhea. Since there is no cure for this disease, you and your

veterinarian will work together to determine the best form of treatment.

Fleas, Ticks, and Mosquitoes

These pests are more than just an annoyance to you and your Cockapoo. They can cause serious diseases if they are not controlled effectively. Safe and effective products are sold through licensed veterinarians and pest control experts, who have been trained and certified, and are controlled by the Environmental Protection Agency. The best way to protect your Cockapoo is with a year-round treatment program. Talk to your veterinarian and pest control expert about the best way to protect your Cockapoo.

Fleas and Ticks Can Cause Serious Problems

Flea allergy dermatitis—This is the most common skin condition for dogs. Severe reactions to flea bites cause itching and a rash. Hair loss and infection are the results of flea allergy. Your veterinarian will prescribe a treatment program to ease the affects of this condition.

Lyme disease—Deer ticks are the main transmitters of Lyme disease. It is a bacterial disease that causes painful disability in humans and dogs. Without treatment, damage to the heart, kidneys, and joints can occur. The tick must remain attached for 24 to 72 hours for the bacteria to be transferred. This gives you time to remove the tick before it can infect your Cockapoo. Antibiotics are prescribed to treat Lyme disease.

Canine ehrlichiosis—This infectious disease is transmitted by an infected brown dog tick. Fever, respiratory distress, weight loss, and bruises are signs of this disease. The prognosis is

TIP

The Correct Way to Remove a Tick

Use forceps or tweezers and wear disposable gloves because ticks can transmit disease to humans through their bodily fluids. Grab the head of the tick, as close to your Cockapoo's body as possible, and pull back with a quick motion. Examine the tick before disposing of it to make sure the head was removed. If you suspect the head is still in your dog's skin, a trip to the veterinarian is necessary. It is normal for a small welt to develop where the tick was removed. Check the area over the next few days for any unusual signs of infection. See your veterinarian, if necessary, to test your Cockapoo for any tick-borne diseases.

good if it is treated in the early stages, so take your Cockapoo to the veterinarian immediately if you suspect he has been infected.

Rocky Mountain spotted fever—The American dog tick and the Rocky Mountain wood tick are the main carriers of this disease. Both humans and dogs can become infected. The organisms are transmitted within several hours of the tick attaching and feeding on the host. Inflammation, joint swelling, difficulty breathing, and coughing may be signs of this disease. Blood tests are administered to confirm the diagnosis and antibiotics are used to treat the illness.

Checking your Cockapoo daily for ticks and fleas is the best preventive measure against these diseases. He should be inspected immediately after walking in the woods, swimming in a lake, visiting a dog park, or playing in high grasses and weeds.

Mosquitoes Transmit Heartworm Larvae

Mosquitoes can cause serious health problems to your Cockapoo. Heartworm disease can be transmitted with just one bite. It is a potentially deadly condition, but, like Lyme disease, it is preventable. The only way dogs can become infected is from the bite of an infected mosquito. However, your Cockapoo may not show signs of infection for up to two years. By then, the disease is difficult and almost impossible to treat. It is a serious and potentially fatal disease, clogging the heart and major blood vessels with adult worms. Using heartworm preventive medicine is the best way to ensure your Cockapoo does not become infected.

Intestinal Parasites—Worms

Why be concerned about worms? Besides the fact that the word itself can make you cringe, just knowing that there are internal parasites possibly roaming through your dog's intestines causing serious problems should be a concern. Then there is the possibility that these worms can also infect humans, so treating and eliminating these parasites is critical. Your veterinarian will do a stool check to screen for worms as part of your Cockapoo's annual checkup.

Signs of Worms

✔ Change in appetite
✔ Distended abdomen
✔ Weakness
✔ Diarrhea or vomiting
✔ Weight loss

✔ Scooting (dragging his rear end across the floor)

Roundworms (*Toxocara canis*)

Roundworms are the most common worms found in dogs. Almost all puppies are born with worms or are infected shortly after birth through nursing. In addition, roundworms can be contracted through contaminated soil or by eating infected rodents. Roundworms feed on digested food, leading to dehydration, intestinal blockage, and even death. Treatment should begin early and continue every two weeks until three months of age. After that, annual testing should be sufficient.

Hookworms (*Ancylostoma caninum*)

Hookworms are parasites that attach themselves to the intestinal wall and suck blood. Your Cockapoo can become infected through contaminated soil or grass. Larvae burrow through the skin, causing inflammation, and migrate to the intestines. Puppies can be born with hookworms or become infected from nursing. A severe infection can cause serious health problems and even death. Your veterinarian will test a stool sample if you suspect your Cockapoo has hookworms.

Tapeworms (*Dipylidium*)

Your Cockapoo can become infected with tapeworms from ingesting a flea that is carrying the tapeworm larva. These worms also live in the intestines. Diarrhea, vomiting, anemia, and weight loss are side effects of tapeworm infection. Tapeworm segments can remain on the rear of your dog after he has had a bowel movement. Your veterinarian will do a fecal test to confirm that tapeworms are present and prescribe a dewormer.

First Aid and Emergency Care

Emergencies can range from serious injury to serious health conditions. Knowing how to handle an emergency can save your Cockapoo's life. Your first priority is to be prepared. Know where the closest emergency clinic is located in case your veterinarian's office does not handle emergency care. Keep a pet first aid kit in your home. These can be purchased or you can create your own. Include the following items in your pet's first aid kit:

✔ Emergency phone numbers—poison control, veterinarian emergency hospital, and your Cockapoo's veterinarian.

✔ Disposal latex gloves

✔ Hydrogen peroxide (3 percent)

✔ Antibiotic ointment for wounds

✔ Benadryl or similar product for allergic reactions

✔ Styptic powder to control nail bleeding

✔ Instant ice pack

✔ Saline solution for flushing eyes

✔ Rolls and pads of gauze in different sizes

✔ Bandage tape

✔ Cortisone spray or cream

✔ Rectal thermometer

✔ Cotton balls

✔ Muzzle

✔ Magnifying glass

✔ Flashlight or penlight

✔ Tweezers or forceps

✔ A heavy beach towel/blanket to use as a stretcher and for warmth

✔ Several cloth and paper towels

✔ Pedialyte for dehydration

✔ Karo syrup for low blood sugar

✔ Heatstroke
✔ Hypothermia
✔ Vomiting blood or diarrhea
✔ Prolonged fever
✔ Paralysis
✔ Poison ingestion
✔ Animal bite wounds

Your veterinarian may suggest other items to keep in your pet's first aid kit.

During an emergency, your objective is to save your dog's life, reduce pain, prevent further injury, and transport him safely to a veterinarian. Try to stay calm—breathe. If you are frantic, confused, or passed out, you cannot effectively help your Cockapoo. You need to make quick decisions. Knowing first aid pet techniques can make the difference between life and death. The American Red Cross offers dog first aid courses and books to help prepare dog owners for an emergency.

When to Seek Emergency Care

If your Cockapoo exhibits any of the following conditions, use your pet's first aid kit, call your veterinarian, and follow his instructions for safely transporting your Cockapoo to the emergency clinic.
✔ Severe or prolonged bleeding
✔ Broken bones
✔ Difficulty breathing
✔ Seizures
✔ Fainting or collapse
✔ Trauma of any kind
✔ Shock
✔ Abdominal pain or bloating

Pet Health Insurance

Most dog owners can afford routine veterinarian expenses—it's the unexpected cancer treatment or vehicular accident care ($3,500–$5,000) that can create a hardship. A fractured bone or knee surgery can cost $2,300 to $3,500. This is when pet insurance can be beneficial. It's a way to keep you from having to make the decision between your Cockapoo's life and your checkbook.

Pet insurance has become more popular among dog owners during the past decade. There are a variety of health plans available—from routine medical expense coverage to only accident and illness coverage. Premiums can be as low as $100 annually depending on the plan selected. Like medical insurance, you are paying for something you may never use. It's a risk you take to make sure you can pay for unexpected medical expenses.

Pet insurance only pays a portion of your veterinarian bills. Most pet insurance companies require that you pay the veterinary bill upfront and then submit the bill to them for reimbursement. It isn't a perfect system yet, but it can provide the peace of mind and security of knowing that unexpected medical treatment for your Cockapoo can be handled, without creating a financial burden. (See the "Information" section for several pet insurance companies.)

SAFETY, PROTECTION, KENNELS, AND DOG SITTERS

Planning ahead and being prepared is the key to keeping your Cockapoo safe when he is out with you, when he is home alone, or when you must be away for several days. This chapter covers a variety of important things you should consider to keep him safe.

Why You Should Microchip

The microchip has an identification number that is entered into a national registry along with contact information for you and your veterinarian. In the event that your pup is lost, a veterinarian or animal control personnel can scan him to get his ID number and contact you. Most breeders and veterinarians can insert a chip under your pup's skin for a nominal fee. It's quite simple and painless. There is a much better chance of bringing your lost pup home if he has a microchip. Many microchip registries offer online services for instant flyers, as well as searchable listings of lost and found pets. Each service charges a fee that varies by amount and membership renewal intervals.

See our information page for microchip company listings.

Missing Cockapoo! Be Prepared

Always have a recent photo of your Cockapoo on hand, especially if you are traveling together. Keep the photo with you to help bystanders recognize him for an immediate search of the area should you discover him missing.

Contact everyone listed below as soon as possible:
✔ Your microchip registry
✔ Local animal control
✔ Canine rescues and shelters

✔ Neighbors, family, and friends
✔ Your veterinarian
  What to include on a flyer:
✔ Recent photo with his name
✔ Description with any special markings
✔ Microchip ID number
✔ Place, day, and time last seen
✔ Medications he takes
✔ Contact information for you and your veterinarian
✔ Reward information if offered
  Places you can distribute flyers:
✔ Your neighbors
✔ Canine rescues and shelters
✔ Local shops and convenience stores
✔ Fire departments
✔ Animal control
✔ Veterinarian offices in your area
✔ School bus drivers
✔ Parks and dog parks

Losing any pet is a terrible experience. Having a plan and working it through will give you some peace of mind in terms of knowing you have done everything you can to find your lost Cockapoo.

Kennels and Dog Sitters

Leaving Your Cockapoo for Hours

At times, it will be necessary to leave your Cockapoo home alone. If left alone in your home to wander from room to room, searching for you and feeling abandoned, your pup is likely to find your favorite pair of running shoes and seek consolation by chewing on one. Have a plan and prepare in advance for those times you must leave your Cockapoo home alone. You can be away with peace of mind and return home to a pup that is glad to see you, not neurotic or insecure.

Your primary concern should be creating a safe place for him to stay. The safe zone explained on page 25 is a good solution. You should be able to take your puppy to the safe zone and leave him there anxiety-free for several hours.

Many professionals use the crate because it offers an emotional sense of safety and comfort. Smaller Cockapoos do extremely well spending extended periods of time in their crates. Owners of larger dogs often feel the crate is too confining for daytime and seek other options, such as the safe zone.

Doggie day care programs are an excellent alternative a couple days a week if you work away from home and your Cockapoo is alone for long hours. But just as with a child's day care, the dog, facility, staff, and patrons will determine whether the experience is enjoyable or stressful. If you have done a good job with socialization, it will more likely be a fun day for your pup. Do your homework and introduce your dog gradually to the day care. Avoid driving up and leaving him alone on the very first visit.

Leaving Your Cockapoo for Days

Just as all breeders are not equal, neither are kennels. With some due diligence on your part, you can kennel your Cockapoo and be free from worry. There are "resorts" and "spas" available as kennel options which offer everything from air conditioned suites with TVs and music to swimming pools and canine massages.

Some offer video monitoring, allowing you to view the suite and activities via the Internet. For most families, a clean, comfortable, and safe kennel that provides daily exercise, playtime, frequent human contact, and protection from other aggressive guests is reasonable enough.

TIP

Before You Leave
- ✔ Be prepared ahead of time.
- ✔ Double check the safe zone.
- ✔ Let neighbors and family know your plans.
- ✔ Post a Pet Alert sticker for fire and emergency personnel.
- ✔ Keep a file with his medical records and any special needs visible.
- ✔ Have your veterinarian's contact information visible.
- ✔ Leave music or TV on to keep your pup company.
- ✔ Leave quickly and quietly.

═══ TIP ═══

For Boarding

✔ Bring feeding instructions and plenty of your pup's food. If your Cockapoo is on a special diet, discuss this with the kennel staff.

✔ Before you take your pup to a kennel, make sure all required canine vaccinations and heartworm medications are up to date.

✔ A good kennel will require medical records for verification.

✔ Be sure to discuss any medications your veterinarian has prescribed, along with instructions for administering them, with the kennel staff.

✔ Bring a favorite toy and blanket or mat.

Kennels

It's a good idea to start looking for a kennel soon after bringing your Cockapoo home. An excellent resource is the *Pet Care Services Association*. Members of the association must adhere to a code of ethics and high standards of facility management. Their website, *www. petcareservices.org*, provides excellent information to assist you in finding good kennels. Your veterinarian may also offer boarding services or be able to make suggestions. Talk to other dog owners you know and ask for recommendations.

The scariest thing you can do to your Cockapoo is drive up to a new kennel and abandon him there for days. Remember, he doesn't know if you are ever coming back. Try to lessen his anxiety by introducing him to the kennel in small steps. Take him on a field trip to tour the facility so he will become familiar with its sights and smells. When you leave him for an overnight, he'll remember your confident energy and smiling face and will hopefully sleep better while you are away.

Isolation is bad for any dog, but for the Cockapoo with such high intelligence and need for human companionship, it is misery. Most kennels offer a menu of services: group play-time, nature walks, individual play sessions with staff members, and field trips to dog parks. These will add to your overall cost, but for your Cockapoo, consider it a necessity.

Dog Sitters

A dog sitter is another option. They will stop by several times a day while you are away. Some take care of everything from mail to pets. The National Association for Professional Pet Sitters

Dog Sitters

✔ Ask for references and call several of the clients.

✔ Ask the sitter to take your Cockapoo on a short walk and observe their interaction.

✔ Establish when to use the safe zone or crate.

✔ Put all your expectations in writing.

✔ Have all feeding and care instructions in writing.

✔ Put your shoes and clothing out of reach.

✔ Ask neighbors to be observant while you are away.

✔ Have a backup plan in case of an emergency.

✔ Leave your dog's vaccination folder and veterinary information in plain view.

(*www.Petsitters.org*) is a good resource. Members become certified by completing special training on pet care, behavior, and nutrition.

Auto Travel Safety

Many owners choose to take their Cockapoos along while running errands, visiting friends, or attending outdoor public events. It's important to keep your pup safe as you travel by auto.

Think of your Cockapoo just as you would a child. The U.S. Department of Health and Human Services requires children under 40 pounds to travel secured in a safety seat located in the rear passenger area. Even if your Cockapoo is the larger standard size, he will likely never exceed 24 pounds.

Traveling in a safety seat or crate is recommended for all Cockapoos. There are many canine auto safety seats and seat belt harnesses on the market to fit any size dog and any budget. When using these, however, your pup can still tumble around during a quick stop or sharp turn. If you choose to keep your Cockapoo in a cargo area, you should still use a crate or safety harness. Experts agree that using a crate provides the best protection.

Never allow your dog to ride in the front seat. Air bags in that area can be deadly or cause serious injuries. If he isn't confined, your pup is likely to climb across your lap while you drive and cause dangerous distractions.

Take water along for your pup. Preparing a travel kit and having your pet first aid kit in the car is highly recommended. In your travel kit, include a copy of your pup's current vaccination record, a recent photo of him, your veterinarian or emergency contact numbers, and an extra leash.

Seeing an adorable Cockapoo "cool breezing" with his head hanging out of the window will definitely make you smile. No matter how cute he looks or how much he loves feeling the wind on his face, don't allow it! You wouldn't allow your child to travel hanging out of the window, so don't let your pup. Dogs can easily jump or fall out of the window, causing deadly injury.

If there is any chance your dog will be left in the car alone, be aware that it takes only 25 minutes for the interior temperature to reach 110°F when the outside temperature is just 78°F. Overheating can be fatal to a dog and hypothermia in cold weather can be just as dangerous. Check weather conditions, consider where you are going, and leave your pup safely at home, rather than taking a chance with his well being.

Your Cockapoo is likely to develop anxiety about approaching and being in the car if he associates a car ride with ending only in an unpleasant trip to the veterinarian, kennel, or groomer. Be sure to take drives that end in something enjoyable, like a walk in the park, a visit to a pet store, seeing friends, and most importantly, returning to his happy home.

Boating and Water Safety

Your Cockapoo will take almost any opportunity to enjoy a lake, stream, pond, creek, puddle, or pool. If you plan to take your pup out into natural environments like hiking trails, parks, campgrounds, or beaches, keep the following things in mind:

Canine Life Jackets

Sturdy adjustable straps and Velcro keep them firmly on your dog, even during the most vigorous jumping and swimming. The handle on the back allows you to reach down and pull your Cockapoo out of the water with ease. There is a ring for attaching a leash to the back, as well.

Water Quality

All natural bodies of water contain varying degrees of microorganisms, parasites, mineral content, and bacteria. If you wouldn't take a plunge in a particular body of water, don't allow your pup to do it. There are risks for infections in the eyes and ears, stomach and digestive problems, and skin irritations.

Moving Water

Many rivers and large creeks are actually moving with a stronger current than they appear to be from the bank. Although Cockapoos are great swimmers, fighting a strong current will quickly tire any pup. It's best to use a tie-out line secured to shore and attached to his life jacket when near or in moving water.

Easy Exit

Make sure your pup has an easy way to get out of the water. Let him practice his exit once or twice before you let him swim freely.

Swimming Pools and Hot Tubs

Cockapoos love swimming pools. Most likely, it is because people share the water with their pup. Covers on pools should fit properly to prevent your pup from entering the water and becoming lost under the canvas. Hot tubs are off limits! Never allow your Cockapoo to enter one unless you keep the temperature down and the jets off.

At the Beach

Salt water is not harmful to dogs and many love bounding through the waves, but others only enjoy fresh water. If your Cockapoo has no interest in the ocean, never force him to enter the water. For both humans and dogs, the surf, undertow, and sea life present the greatest possibility for injury.

Make sure you have an adequate supply of fresh water on hand for hydration. The sun can be as harsh on your pup as it is on you. Provide him shade during the heat of the day. After leaving the beach, check your pup's paws for sand between his toes. Rub a generous amount of Vaseline or paw wax on the pads of his feet to prevent soreness and restore the surface. Hot sand can be brutal on tender paw pads.

Boats

Regardless of what type of boat you have, a life jacket is a must for your Cockapoo. Your pup may surprise you by jumping overboard when you least expect it. Use a tether at all times when the boat is motoring.

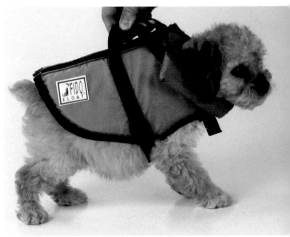

HOW-TO: MAKE A

Devastating natural or man-made disasters can affect our lives unexpectedly. Whether tornados, hurricanes, floods, fires, blizzards, or terrorism strike, we need to be prepared. Pet owners have learned from past disaster experiences that planning ahead can save a lot of beloved pets from becoming lost or perishing.

During Hurricane Katrina, President George W. Bush said that if he had to evacuate one thing, he would take his dog Barney. On October 6, 2006, the president signed the Pets Evacuation and Transportation Standards (PETS) Act into law to help ensure that America's pets and service animals would not be left behind in a disaster.

Five national organizations have joined forces to help you in planning to protect your Cockapoo. The five organizations are the Department of Homeland Security, the American Kennel Club, the Humane Society of the United States, the American Veterinary Medical Association, and the American Society for the Prevention of Cruelty to Animals. See our "Information" section to get contact details for each of these organizations and visit *www.ready.gov,* their consolidated disaster planning website.

You should be prepared for three possible emergency circumstances.

A Personal Emergency

Fire breaks out in your own home or you are hospitalized for an injury while away from home.

Post a "Save My Pet" decal at all entry doors. These are available at many pet stores and online from a variety of suppliers and pet organizations. The ASPCA provides them free of charge. Visit *www.aspca.org* to request one. Some decals allow you to indicate how many pets are at home and include your phone number for emergency responders.

Create a "Pet Emergency Contact" list to post in a conspicuous place, such as the refrigerator. It should include the following items:

✔ Where you can be reached throughout a typical day
✔ A local contact person in case you are not available
✔ Your local veterinarian, pharmacy, and boarding kennel
✔ Your pup's microchip number

Assemble a "Pet Emergency Information" kit and include the following items:

✔ Current copies of your Cockapoo's vaccination records

✔ A recent photo of you together with him
✔ Proof of ownership and your Pet Emergency Contact list
✔ Include a labeled three-day supply of any medications with instructions
✔ An extra leash and collar
✔ Your pup's feeding schedule, including what not to feed him in case of allergies

Put these items in a sturdy container and mark it boldly with his name and "Pet Emergency Information." When you leave him home alone, place it in plain sight, where rescuers or neighbors will notice it quickly.

A Local or Community Emergency

Events like tornados or wildfires strike. Prepare a "Pet Emergency Supply" kit separate from any kits you may have for your family. Include the "Pet Emergency Information" kit described above. In the event that you are not at home, rescuers can take this kit along with your pup to a shelter. If you are at home, but electrical and water services are not restored, and your ability to travel is limited, this kit will take care of your pup's needs until help arrives or you are able to leave the area.

Include these items in your "Pet Emergency Supply" kit:

✔ Two-week supply of food (Canned food is recommended due to its high water content.)
✔ One-week supply of water in plastic bottles
✔ Crate or carrier (labeled with your Cockapoo's name and your contact information)
✔ Manual can opener and spoon for canned food
✔ Familiar items to make him feel comfortable (favorite toys, treats, blankets)
✔ Canine first aid kit
✔ One-week supply of prescriptions labeled with instructions
✔ A reasonable waste disposal system (newspaper, puppy training pads, paper towels, dog poop bags)
✔ Waterless bath shampoo, pre-moistened wipes, and a grooming brush
✔ Bowls for food and water
✔ Stakes and tie-outs

A National or Regional Emergency

These result in large-scale evacuations.

In an emergency when local evacuation may be necessary, your kennel, veterinarian, or rescue shelters are usually able to assist you with temporary pet care arrangements. It's the large-scale emergencies that pose the greatest challenges to pet owners and rescue workers alike.

During a large-scale emergency, you may be faced with a possible 90-mile or out-of-state mandatory evacuation order. It could be weeks, days, or even several months before life returns to normal. By following these three recommendations, you will be well prepared for a large-scale evacuation.

If you are ordered to evacuate, never leave your Cockapoo tied up. *Always* take your dog with you if possible. The Emergency Supply kit

you prepared according to the directions above will contain everything you need for your pup.

There are many "pet-friendly" hotels for people who travel with their canine companions. Take time before the unexpected occurs to search out places you can go where pets are welcome. Explore *www.TripswithPets.com*, an online resource that provides information by state on hotels and short-term rental homes that allow pets. Begin calling for a reservation as soon as you anticipate a possible evacuation order. These types of properties fill up quickly.

If you are going to a public shelter, be aware that dogs are not permitted at these facilities; however, thanks to the Pets Evacuation and Transportation Act (PETS), the Federal Emergency Management Agency (FEMA) now has a program to keep them protected, as well. The plan provides self-contained mobile command centers that coordinate the care, housing, and restoration of our beloved pets back to their families. In an emergency, FEMA will direct you where to deliver your pup and his supply kit.

INFORMATION

Clubs

American Cockapoo Club
Taylors, SC, Phone: (864) 895-5721
www.americancockapooclub.com

American Canine Hybrid Club
Harvey, AR, Phone: (479) 299-4415
www.achclub.com

American Kennel Club
Raleigh, NC, Phone: (919) 233-9767
www.akc.org

Kennel Club UK
Piccadilly London, Phone: 0 (870) 606-6750
www.thekennelclub.org.uk

United Kennel Club
Kalamazoo, MI, Phone: (269) 343-9020
www.ukcdogs.com

Veterinary Associations

Academy of Veterinary Homeopathy
Wilmington, DE, Phone: (866) 652-1590
www.theavh.org

American Animal Hospital Association
Denver, CO, Phone: (303) 986-1780
www.aahanet.org

American Veterinary Chiropractic Association
Bluejacket, OK, Phone: (918) 784-2231
www.animalchiropractic.org

American Veterinary Medical Association
Schaumburg, IL, Phone: (847) 925-1329
www.avma.org

Emergency Preparedness

Department of Homeland Security Pet Info
www.ready.gov

Federal Emergency Management Association
Washington, DC, Phone: (800) 462-7585
www.fema.gov

Humane Society of the United States
Washington, DC, Phone: (202) 452-1100
www.hsus.org

Poison Hotlines

Animal Poison Hotline
Phone: (888) 232-8870

ASPCA Animal Poison Control Center
Phone: (888) 426-4435
www.aspca.org/pet-care/poison-control

Pet Poison Helpline
Phone: (800) 213-6680
www.petpoisonhelpline.com

Canine Training

Association of Pet Dog Trainers
Greenville, SC, Phone: (800) 738-3647
www.apdt.com

Certification Council for Professional
    Dog Trainers
New York, NY, Phone: (212) 356-0682
www.ccpdt.org

The International School for Dog Trainers
Monteverde, FL, Phone: (407) 469-5583
www.internationaldogschool.com/index.html

National Association of Dog Obedience
  Instructors
Hurst, TX
www.nadoi.org/

Groomer Associations
International Professional Groomers, Inc.
Elk Grove Village, IL, Phone: (847) 758-1938
www.ipgcmg.org

International Society of Canine Cosmetologists
Garland, TX
www.petstylist.com

National Dog Groomers Association of
  America, Inc.
Clark, PA, Phone: (724) 962-2711
www.nationaldoggroomcrs.com

Microchip Registries
American Kennel Club Companion Animal
  Recovery
Raleigh, NC, Phone: (800) 252-7894
www.akccar.org/

Avid ID Systems, Inc. (USA)
Norco, CA, Phone: (951) 371-7505
www.avidid.com

HomeAgain
Kenilworth, NJ, Phone: (888) 466-3242
www.HomeAgain.com

Organizations
American Red Cross National Headquarters
Washington, DC, Phone: (202) 303-5000
www.redcross.org

American Society for the Prevention of
  Cruelty to Animals (ASPCA)
New York, NY, Phone: (212) 876-7700
www.aspca.org

Association of American Feed Control Officials
  (AAFCO)
http://www.aafco.org

Pet Insurance
Hartville Group
Canton, OH, Phone: (866) 820-7764
www.hartvillegroup.com

Pethealth, Inc.
Underwritten by Lincoln General Insurance
  Company
Phone: (866) 275-7387
www.pethealthinc.com

Pet Partners Healthcare Plan Inc.
Raleigh, NC, Phone: (877) 738-7888
www. iafbph.com

Pet Protect, Inc.
Naples, FL, Phone: (239) 403-4100
www.pethealthinsure.com

National Casualty Company
Brea, CA, Phone: (888) 899-4VPI
http://www.petinsurance.com

Other Helpful Resources
National Association of Professional Pet Sitters
Mt. Laurel, NJ, Phone: (856) 439-0525
www.petsitters.org

Pet Care Services Association
Colorado Springs, CO, Phone: (877) 570-7788
www.tripswithpets.com

Petfinder, A Discovery Company
www.petfinder.com

Trips with Pets
South Portland, ME
www.TripswithPets.com

Therapy Dogs, Inc.
Cheyenne, WY, Phone: (877) 843-7364
www.TherapyDogs.com

United States Dog Agility Association
Richardson, TX, Phone: (972) 487-2200
www.usdaa.com

United States Department of Agriculture
FDA Animal Veterinary Association
Silver Spring, MD, Phone: (888) 463-6332
http://www.fda.gov/AnimalVeterinary

INDEX

About the Authors

Writing under the pen name of Erin Amon: Laura Johnson, Eden Purdy, and Tana Riddell are freelance writers and sisters who specialize in the care and behavior of Poodle hybrid dogs. Blending together their writing skills from successful business careers, and as hybrid dog owners for over thirty years, they provide personal knowledge and experience to readers who seek more information about these unique pets. They reside in Georgia with their Cockapoos, Yorkipoos, and Lhasapoos.

As owners and operators of Three Sisters Enterprises, LLC, the sisters maintain a website marketing hybrid specialty products and are currently working on a series of books to educate dog lovers about the characteristics of Poodle designer dogs.

Acknowledgments

Special thanks go to the following people for providing insight and guidance on the content of this book: Linda Zarro, President of the American Cockapoo Club; Doris Dressler, certified service dog trainer and owner of LuvsK9s.com; Graham Carroll, DVM, Tigertown Vet; Miranda Spindel, President Association of Shelter Veterinarians; and a very special thank you to our families for their continuous support and to God, who makes all things possible.

Important Note

This pet owner's manual tells the reader how to buy or adopt and care for a Cockapoo. The author and the publisher consider it important to point out that the advice given in the book is meant primarily for normally developed dogs of excellent physical health and sound temperament.

Anyone who acquires a fully-grown dog should be aware that the animal has already formed its basic impressions of human beings. The new owner should watch the animal carefully, including its behavior toward humans, and, whenever possible, should meet the previous owner.

Caution is further advised in the association of children with dogs, in meeting with other dogs, and in exercising the dog without a leash.

Even well-behaved and carefully supervised dogs can sometimes damage property or cause accidents. It is therefore in the owner's interest to be adequately insured against such eventualities, and we strongly urge all dog owners to purchase a liability policy that also covers their dog.

Cover Photos

Jean Fogle: back cover; Liz Kaye: front cover; www.LittleFriendsPhoto.com: inside front cover; Shutterstock: inside back cover.

Photo Credits

Norvia Behling: page 6; Jean Fogle: pages 4, 11, 13, 15, 21, 38, 39, 42, 43, 56, 57, 62, 65, 66, 68, 74, 77, 80, 84, 86, 87 (top); Kent Dannen: pages 12, 33, 55; Isabelle Francais: page 7; Paulette Johnson: pages 2–3, 10, 14, 17, 18, 22, 24, 25, 28, 31, 34, 35, 37, 45, 47, 48, 50, 51, 58, 63, 71, 78, 87 (bottom), 91, 92; Liz Kaye: pages 9, 19, 27, 69, 81, 83; www.LittleFriendsPhoto.com: page 60; Pets by Paulette: pages 5, 32, 40, 41, 54, 61, 72, 82; Shutterstock: pages 64, 67.

All inquiries should be addressed to:
Barron's Educational Series, Inc.
250 Wireless Boulevard
Hauppauge, NY 11788
www.barronseduc.com

ISBN-13: 978-0-7641-4020-4
ISBN-10: 0-7641-4020-5

Library of Congress Control Number: 2009038030

Library of Congress Cataloging-in-Publication Data
Amon, Erin.
    Cockapoos: everything about purchase, care, nutrition, behavior, and training / Erin Amon.
        p. cm.
    Included bibliographical references and index.
    ISBN-13: 978-0-7641-4020-4 (alk. paper)
    ISBN-10: 0-7641-4020-5 (alk. paper)
    1. Cockapoo. I. Title.
    SF429. C54A46 2010
    636.72—dc22   2009038030

Printed in China
9 8 7 6 5